Critical Choice in Times of Crisis

The Book of Ruth

Carol Gwynne

Grosvenor House
Publishing Limited

This book is published by
Grosvenor House Publishing Ltd
Link House
140 The Broadway, Tolworth, Surrey, KT6 7HT.
www.grosvenorhousepublishing.co.uk

A CIP record for this book
is available from the British Library

ISBN 978-1-83975-449-4

Dedication

To Hannah, my granddaughter who was miraculously healed of a rare childhood cancer. She jumped all the hurdles in her life with faith, hope, fortitude and strength, which led to a successful career, health and fulfilment.

To you, the reader, for unknowingly supporting the destitute through the purchase of this book.

Acknowledgements

D R. Steve Selby, who would have known a phone call from you some three years ago would ignite my passion to write this book. I am so grateful for your excellent advice and guidance throughout my years of study at Trinity.

Linda Stubblefield, for your patience, love and encouragement. For the memorable fellowship we share, and the work you did from proofreading to publication of this book.

Hannah Miles, who captured my vision and designed the cover.

Diana and Eva, thank you for your prayers and for sharing your poignant journey.

My extended family across the globe from different cultures, race and faith for enriching my life.

Table of Contents

Foreword

D R. GWYNNE WRITES, "Buried deep in the text of Ruth is a message of hope to all people, that even in the most dire and bleakest moments in life, comfort and restoration is to be found in God, who is able to give more than we can imagine."

This book is a rare blend of scholarship, spiritual insight, personal struggle and current practical application that draws the reader both intellectually and emotionally into this wondrous biblical account like never before.

Dr. Gwynne first carefully explains the biblical historical context of the narrative so that the reader can view the account through the eyes of the participants. After carefully introducing and explaining each event in the narrative, she then dips deep into the spiritual concepts that these events illustrate such as *hesedh* (love, loyalty and faithfulness). Readers are then taken to other passages of Scripture from both the Old and New Testaments to further illustrate and codify these spiritual concepts.

Finally, her willingness to share her personal struggles and ultimate triumph with issues of faith, disappointments and even tragic loss adds a personal touch that brings the concepts truly alive and illustrates the practical applications to today's world.

I am confident every reader will find a wealth of fresh understanding and present-day application of these wonderful Scriptures.

– Dr. Steve Selby
Enrollment Services Director
Trinity College of the Bible and Theological Seminary
Evansville, Indiana

Introduction

THE BOOK OF Ruth is a timeless story recalled through the generations as one of comfort in times of despair, instilling into the reader the divine providence of Almighty God throughout the ages.

It is critical to bear in mind that Ruth was not written to accommodate the mindset of present-day readers and thus should be read against its historical and theological background. Several concepts, themes or motifs point to a network of Old Testament texts and aspects of Judaism that the contemporaneous audience would have readily understood.

However, inasmuch as the book was and still is sacred writings to those of the Jewish faith, the same applies to Christians in the twenty-first century. Ruth is by no means a simple romantic story from centuries past. On the contrary, the faith, trust and actions of the protagonists should be viewed as divine examples of how to lead fulfilled lives in this day and age. Notable is the constant action of prayer and selfless giving.

These principles of faith apply greatly to present situations, particularly to a needy world. The outflowing of grace and love demonstrated by Naomi, Ruth and Boaz sets an excellent manifesto for all mankind to practise. Additionally, the narrative reinforces the promise that even in the depths of despair the Lord saves and will never forsake us.[1]

Many Christians and other religions are being led by false doctrines and as a result lack the life-giving promises of God. Every person on earth will at one time or another experience a major crisis. A spiritually bankrupt person at a time of need has nothing to draw from. The promises of man will not suffice. It brings to mind the rebuke of our Lord through the prophet Hosea: *"My people are destroyed for lack of knowledge."*[2]

The eighty-five verses contained within four chapters in Ruth are laced with intricacies and divinely inspired guidance discerned by the words and actions of the protagonists that are applicable in our daily lives. The narrative addresses human failings, the pain of tragedy, widowhood, obedience, loving kindness and fulfilment and, most importantly, faith in Almighty God who is able to give more than we could ever hope for.

The essence of this book is to explore the rich theological implications in simplistic language that may be readily understood by both Christians and non-Christians who hitherto have viewed Ruth as a simple love story of a poor girl who got lucky and married a rich old man! Hopefully, these writings will encourage and guide you, the reader, towards leading a fulfilled life and to stand firm in your faith when faced with what seems to be an impossible or tragic situation.

When read intertextually, my hope is that you will have a greater understanding of God's nature and divine providence throughout the ages and its relevance today. The story of Ruth is not restricted to Judaism and Christianity but also reaches outwards towards a darkened malignant world in great need of love and mercy.

Within this short story, the narrator has skilfully woven the supernatural, that is, the subtlety of divine providence into the lives and actions of very ordinary people, which Ronald Hals encapsulates as the "hiddenness" of God.[3] It is not Ruth, Naomi or Boaz, but God who is the key player in this story. Ruth's extraordinary love, compassion, loyalty, obedience and faithfulness, coupled with similar acts of compassion, prayer, love and faithfulness demonstrated by Naomi and Boaz determined Yahweh's will and purpose.

The all causality of God is discerned at every turn of events by the actions of Naomi, Ruth and Boaz. None of the three protagonists had divine visitations, prophetic words, visions, church gatherings, or a priest or a rabbi to pray for them. Factually, it was only Naomi and Boaz who verbalised blessings. The protagonists possessed a vibrant faith and trust in Yahweh based on sound doctrine.

For the modern reader, the narrative provides a paradigm of unshakable faith in times of crisis and also a reminder that even in the darkest tunnel of life, God is more than able to sustain and do the impossible of turning lives around from barrenness to fulfilment.

The prayers said by Naomi and Boaz were not begging, self-centred or an attempt to "control" God; rather, they were ones of continuous praise of Yahweh and the bestowing of blessings on one another.

Although no prayers were recorded as being said by Ruth, her faith was manifested by acts of love and mercy that went beyond moral obligations. Ruth's relationship with Naomi and vice versa, the compassion shown by Boaz, and the acceptance of Ruth by the people transcend all boundaries and manmade obstacles. Ruth was able to move according to the will of God, simply because she was in a close relationship with Yahweh.

Ruth serves as a reminder that the God of Israel is also a God to all humankind. The chasm that exists between race, colour, creed, poverty and wealth stems from an individual's sinful nature and not God's will. As Roy Matheson states: "His wing span is large enough to embrace not only people of the covenant but those like Ruth who enter from the outside."[4]

Ruth is an assurance that God is faithful to His promises irrespective of what, whom or where mankind stands currently. The historical evidence in the Old and New Testament is valid proof that Almighty God *(El Shaddai)* does not renege on His promises and that truth stands today. No matter how bleak the future may seem, no matter what tragic circumstance we are in, God can and does turn things around. *"God causes all things to work together for good to those who love God, to those who are called according to His purpose."*[5]

The key to knowing God's revealed will and purpose is to be found in the Bible. The Bible writers were divinely inspired by the Holy Spirit to record historical events that actually took place to demonstrate divine activity working through faith. Through the agency of the Holy Spirit, as these events are retold, God's will is revealed and the past effects are activated into our present-day lives.

All of Scripture speaks into our everyday lives.[6] For instance, we are called to love, to be kind to our enemies and to bless them.[7] Anxiety causes depression;[8] when anxiety overcomes us, we can seek God's help, who promises we will experience peace beyond our understanding.[9] At all times we should go about our daily tasks even unpleasant ones without complaining[10] and serve one another with love.[11]

Ruth is the perfect revelation of transforming grace that comes from a life of love, selflessness and obedience. We have a faithful omniscient God who never changes.[12] God's intervention in the bleakest of times in generations past is ever-present today.

To be noted, throughout the entire narrative, Yahweh's direct intervention is portrayed only twice. The first marks the turning point of a tragic situation, in that Yahweh had graciously provided food, and the famine had ended in Judah.[13] The second intervention happened when Yahweh gave conception to Ruth.[14] However, throughout the narrative, God's guidance and providence is evident.

The Lord's direct interventions form the inclusion within which we see human actions that bring divine blessings. All three protagonists walked in obedience, and the *Shema*[15] would have been ever-present in their hearts and minds, flowing naturally and guiding their emotions, words and actions.

The first part of the Shema is to be found in Deuteronomy 6:4-9: *"Hear, O Israel: The LORD our God, the LORD is one! You shall love the LORD your God with all your heart, and with all your soul and with all your strength."*[16]

Our Lord Jesus, when questioned by a lawyer as to what is the greatest commandment, responded in this manner: *"You*

*shall love the Lord your God with all your heart and with all
your soul and with all your mind. This is the great and first commandment. And the second is "You shall love your neighbour as
yourself."*[17]

At times some of us may not be able to "love ourselves" and
feel devoid of all emotions, then we should do what Jesus said:
*"A new commandment I give to you, that you love one another;
as I have loved you, that you also love one another"*[18] His love
for us was totally and absolutely self-sacrificial.

The law of love must be written in the hearts of all believers;
it is the very foundation of our faith, as well as the unmet need
of all humanity. Failure to observe these three great comman-
dants will result in self-destruction and that of other lives. Ruth
sets the perfect example to rid oneself of self-centredness, and
we can all draw from her example on the practice of *hesedh*—
both within and without the church.

Hesedh

Hesedh is the highly regarded Hebrew term used to describe
God's unmerited love in the divine-human act of loving kindness, compassion, mercy, love and faithfulness, particularly in
terms of salvation and redemption. For humanity, it is not a
feeling, but rather one of action, an act of giving and expecting
nothing in return. The concept of *hesedh* seen throughout the
narrative is an absolute necessity for all humanity to practice
both in times of peace and disaster.[19]

The narrative opens with disobedience and death, but as
the story progresses, darkness begins to lift because of the ini-

tiatives taken by Ruth, an "outsider." Ruth's choice, coupled with actions of extraordinary love, loyalty and faithfulness, triggered a whole series of events culminating in extraordinary blessings. Naomi and Boaz were also participants in similar acts of love and loyalty. The Hebrew term *hesedh* succinctly encapsulates the tremendous acts of compassion and love demonstrated by the protagonists, which is the central concept within the narrative.

The emotions, events and perceptions in Ruth identify with men and women, young and old, and resonate with problems encountered in life. Buried deep in the text of Ruth is a message of hope to all people, even in the bleakest and most dire moments in life. Comfort and restoration is to be found in God, who is able to give more than we can imagine. However, it does require obedience to and knowledge of God's revealed will as found in the Bible.

The action taken by Ruth, Naomi and Boaz is a perfect example of what it means to have a close relationship with God, out of which naturally flow love, mercy and compassion for others. Making the right choices at a time of crisis is akin to a prayer often said: "thy will be done, thy Kingdom come." Naomi and Ruth did not look at the problem but at the promises of Yahweh.

Ruth in Judaism

In Judaism Ruth was and still is recited on Shavuot. Originally, it was an agricultural festival to celebrate the end of the grain harvest, the feast of the "first fruits." The feast is twofold and of two natures.[20] The double nature refers to the covenants that God made with Noah and with Abraham.[21]

It was called Pentecost by the Hellenistic Jews and "falls seven weeks" (hence, "weeks") or on the fiftieth day (hence, "Pentecost") after the second day of Passover."[22] It is interesting to note that Solomon Zeitlin emphatically states that Shavuot has not the connotation of "weeks" but means *oaths*.[23]

According to the Pentateuch, Shavuot was to be celebrated seven weeks following the offering of the Omer.[24]This idea of "counting" each day represents the life of a Jewish person's spiritual preparation for the acceptance of the Torah into his or her life.[25]

Various reasons are given for the traditional reading of Ruth. Ruth's act of faith and commitment to Judaism is considered analogous to the receiving of the Torah. According to David Ibn Yachia, the reading of Ruth serves as a reminder that "the Torah was given only through affliction and poverty."[26]

Naomi and Ruth entered Bethlehem at the beginning of the barley harvest; thus, events told in the book of Ruth span a period of some fifty-two days from Passover to Shavuot. Ruth became a model for future proselytes as her acceptance of Yahweh symbolised Israel's acceptance of the Torah. Her loyalty to Naomi symbolised Israel's devotion to its vows, and David is said to have died during Shavuot. "All these elements helped no doubt to consecrate Ruth to Shavuot."[27]

The reading of Ruth on Shavuot also serves as a reminder of the expected Messiah, who will arise through the lineage of David. Here then exists the cleavage between Judaism and

Christianity. In Judaism the promise is yet to come; but in Christianity, the fulfilment of the promise is to be found in Christ Jesus who is the Messiah.[28]

Judaism interpreted the Old Testament on the basis of the Torah as governed by the rabbis. A commonality does exist in that there is one God who made Himself known in Israel's history. However, it is absolutely unnecessary to denigrate Judaism in order to affirm Christianity; it is well to remember that the roots of Christianity are to be found in Judaism.

The Book of Ruth
Chapter One

Now it came about in the days when the judges governed, that there was a famine in the land. And a certain man of Bethlehem in Judah went to sojourn in the land of Moab with his wife and his two sons.

2. The name of the man was Elimelech, and the name of his wife, Naomi; and the names of his two sons were Mahlon and Chilion, Ephrathites of Bethlehem in Judah. Now they entered the land of Moab and remained there.

3. Then Elimelech, Naomi's husband, died; and she was left with her two sons.

4. They took for themselves Moabite women as wives; the name of the one was Orpah and the name of the other Ruth. And they lived there about ten years.

5. Then both Mahlon and Chilion also died, and the woman was bereft of her two children and her husband.

6. Then she arose with her daughters-in-law that she might return from the land of Moab, for she had heard in the land of Moab that the LORD had visited His people in giving them food.

7. So she departed from the place where she was, and her two daughters-in-law with her; and they went on the way to return to the land of Judah.

8. And Naomi said to her two daughters-in-law, "Go, return

each of you to her mother's house. May the LORD deal kindly with you as you have dealt with the dead and with me.

9. May the LORD grant that you may find rest, each in the house of her husband." Then she kissed them, and they lifted up their voices and wept.

10. And they said to her, "No but we will surely return with you to your people."

11. But Naomi said, "Return, my daughters. Why should you go with me? Have I yet sons in my womb, that they may be your husbands?

12. Return, my daughters! Go, for I am too old to have a husband. If I said I have hope, if I should even have a husband tonight and also bear sons,

13. would you therefore wait until they were grown? Would you therefore refrain from marrying? No, my daughters; for it is harder for me than for you, for the hand of the LORD has gone forth against me.

14. And they lifted up their voices and wept again; and Orpah kissed her mother-in-law, but Ruth clung to her.

15. Then she said, "Behold, your sister-in-law has gone back to her people and her gods; return after your sister-in-law."

16. But Ruth said, "Do not urge me to leave you or turn back from following you; for where you go, I will go and where you lodge, I will lodge. Your people shall be my people, and your God, my God.

17. Where you die, I will die, and there I will be buried. Thus may the LORD do to me, and worse, if anything but death parts you and me."

18. When she saw that she was determined to go with her, she said no more to her.

19. So they both went until they came to Bethlehem. And when they had come to Bethlehem, all the city was stirred because of them, and the women said, "Is this Naomi?"

20. She said to them, "Do not call me Naomi; call me Mara, for the Almighty has dealt very bitterly with me.

21. I went out full, but the LORD has brought me back empty. Why do you call me Naomi, since the LORD has witnessed against me and the Almighty has afflicted me?"

22. So Naomi returned, and with her Ruth the Moabitess, her daughter-in-law, who returned from the land of Moab. And they came to Bethlehem at the beginning of barley harvest.[29]

~

The Judges

All suggestions by scholars to date the book of Ruth have proven to be inconclusive. Biblically, Ruth is rooted in a specific historical period: *"In the days when the judges ruled."* The opening scene is one of absolute horror followed by famine, disobedience, death, infertility, poverty and utter desolation.

Historically, prior to his death, Joshua exhorted the Israelites to remain faithful to Yahweh and not to involve themselves with pagans and idolatry (Joshua 23:1-7). Following the general conquest of Canaan, the Israelites failed to drive out the inhabitants. As a result, the new generation of Israelites soon forgot the ways of their ancestors who had walked in obedience to the Lord's command.[30]

The younger generation of Israelites were increasingly attracted by the lifestyle of the pagans and began to worship and serve the gods of Baal and Ashtoreth.[31] Following the death of Joshua and the high priest Eleazar, the last link with Moses and Aaron was severed, "and a new era will soon find the Israelites in spiritual decline. Never again will the Israelites as a nation be this closely united, either amongst themselves or with their God."[32]

The Lord in His great mercy, love and compassion raised up judges to rescue the Israelites from oppression and to assist them in warfare, yet they refused to obey and continued to walk in disobedience. As soon as a judge died, "the people returned to their corrupt ways, behaving worse than those who had lived before them."[33]

Thus, the era of the judges was one of repeated disobedience. In the downward spiral of the judges, the rule ends with rape and the dismembering of a Levite's concubine that culminated in intertribal warfare.[34] As a result, all, with the exception of six hundred men, of the Benjamite tribe were murdered, which caused great concern amongst the Israelites that the Benjamite tribe would be "cut off."[35] Their solution for the preservation of the tribe was through violence, murder and the kidnapping of virgins, who were forced to marry the Benjamites.[36]

Theocracy had long been forgotten,[37] and *"Everyone did what was right in his own eyes."*[38] Indeed, as Younger observes: "in an almost unbelievable manner, the problem between one man and one woman leads to a full-scale civil war.[39]

Neither the Levite nor his concubine is named in Judges chapter 19.

The anonymity of this section also reflects the disintegration of an individual's value as a human being. It denies individuality and humanity to both the criminals and victims in the story. Thus the use of anonymity for the characters...proves reinforcement for the portrayal of a malignant fallen world.[40]

The Twenty-First Century

The comment by Younger that "we live in a malignant fallen world" was made in 2006. In an almost unbelievable manner now in the twenty-first century, an increase in violence, mass murders, dismembering of human beings, rape, kidnapping and the enticement of teenagers to join evil is a daily global disaster.

In 2019, Harry Vaughan, an A-star grammar school student was arrested for being a neo-Nazi. Police discovered various documents on Satanism, bomb-making manuals, guides to killing and two videos of child abuse, which were classed as category A. In mitigation, his barrister said: "He is somebody who has disappeared down a rabbit hole, a rabbit hole of the Internet and he is in a very dark place."[41]

Not much has changed except for the increase of evil that has existed since Creation, which reinforces the fact that we live in a fallen malignant world where even the name of God is uttered before the crime. World leaders who profess Christianity have ignored the moral will of God in wanting to preserve their popularity and positions as leaders.

Many profess to be Christians, yet they fail themselves by continuing to follow their own precepts—chasing contemporary idols in their perception of life rather than committing themselves to faith and trust in God. Disobedience to God's precepts in the name of what the public demands is abominable.[42] Sounds familiar to when the public demanded Jesus to be crucified! It just goes to demonstrate the condition of the world today.

Note the desire to preserve a tribe is not dissimilar to that of current Islamist terrorism desiring to have an Islamic state and the will to murder as a means to their end. Mass murder and the dismembering of people is not something of the past, but a present-day reality that needs to be addressed, not by violent retaliation but by educating the ignorant or unstable individual. There is an urgent need for all people despite their religious beliefs to strive for harmony and to live peaceably with one another.

Islamist terrorists appropriating the name of "Allah" have murdered thousands in the hope of establishing caliphates. Many young Muslims and converts have abandoned families to join them in pursuit of what they believe to be a better life.

Their murderous theology is not derived from the Koran. Mohamed K. Jasser in his translation of the Koran states:

The idea of war to produce belief or conversion is never permitted in the Koran...Also in support of free choice in Islam, the Koran says: The truth is from your Lord. One who wants to believe can do so, and one who does not can deny.[43]

Jihad should be a non-violent movement, beginning with self-examination of the heart before Almighty God. In Islam the most recited prayer is "Bismillah-ir-Rahman-ir-Rahim."[44] It must be understood in terms of Allah who is a God of love, mercy and compassion and bestows these divine attributes on his followers. In turn believers are to demonstrate these attributes to one another.

An individual who declares the Muslim prayer of faith or declares Allah is the greatest (Arabic term: *Allah hu Akbar*) then proceeds to murder the innocent and themselves is definitely at odds and in total disobedience and rebellion against Islam. Believing the act of murder and suicide is the route to heaven is delusional. To walk contrary to the declaration of faith is not the path of Islam.

It is not only the Jihadist who murder. Lizzie Dearden reported: "Several children have been killed in the UK as a result of horrific abuse meted out by guardians who believed they were possessed or witches, including an eight-year-old girl who was tortured and a fifteen-year-old boy who drowned during an exorcism."[45]

In 2019, Maggie Smythe was murdered by her ex-partner. Parts of her body were discovered under rubble, but her head was never found.[46] More recently, an almost daily occurrence of horrific and senseless murders is being committed within family units. These murderers have made their presence known on the world stage of evil.

Social media and its dark sites have resulted in young people committing suicide. Satan and his cohorts are evil spirits, and they will seek and inhabit anyone who opens the door of their heart to assist demons to steal, kill and destroy.[47]

We have seen and heard and are still seeing and hearing of all forms of violence, political and religious wars, not merely limited to a country, a religion or a region, but worldwide destruction.

What does emerge in the actions of these poor misguided individuals is the need of security, significance and love (agapé). These basically emotionally, mentally and spiritually unstable ones have fallen into the snare of falsehood leading to demonic instincts. In experiencing a lack of support and love, they pursue evil ideals or unhealthy lifestyles that cannot be sustained and are in direct opposition to all that God has commanded in order to live a peaceful life.

Famine

The book of Ruth nestles between Judges and Samuel as Israel moved from theocracy to a monarchy. Ruth is like a brilliant diamond shining out of the desolation of violence, disobedience and idolatry. Ruth's love, loyalty and faith serves as a sharp reminder not only to the listeners of her time, but also call to us now in the twenty-first century to live out our faith in obedience to God, to love Him above all else, and to keep moving outwards in love and action for others.

———

Against the tragic background of the Judges, famine strikes the land. Ironically, Bethlehem means "house of bread." The narrator gave no reason as to the cause of famine in Bethlehem. However, the mention of famine would cause the audience to reflect on past biblical patterns of famine.[48]

Historically, despite tragic circumstances, God's redemptive plans for His people were not and will not be thwarted.[49] Outstanding is the story of Joseph, who was sold into slavery by his brothers.[50] In fact, even in this day and age, tragic circumstances often advance God's plan for all humanity.

Famine was associated with God's judgment as outlined in Leviticus 26 and Deuteronomy 28. Perhaps it was to serve as a counterpoint to the era of the Judges as the story moves from one of disobedience to obedience, mercy, loving kindness, and fulfilment. No one really knows the reason for the famine, even if it had been caused by drought from the lack of rain, it is well to remember that God controls even the rain to further His cause!

Yahweh did send famines because of persistent disobedience. For instance, when God struck Samaria with famine, drought, plagues and locusts, He did so because of wild living, cruelty to the poor, and idolatry, which is tantamount to disobedience.[51] Today the average family and the privileged may not encounter a lack of food, but spiritual famine can be devastating.

The apostle Paul makes clear historical events were divinely recorded as a warning for us today:

"These things happened to them as examples for us. If you think you are standing strong, be careful not to fall.

———

The temptations in your life are no different from what others experience. And God is faithful."[52]

Idolatry goes beyond the normal mindset of one praying to different gods or indulging in so-called forms of attaining levels of *karma*. It is seeking happiness and security from idle words of human beings or from material things, which cannot satisfy and draw the created away from the Creator. Disobedience of any kind is rebellion against God and is a sin; with sin comes death. However, no matter how great the sin, with repentance comes forgiveness and new life.

In Revelation 3:20 Jesus says: *"Behold, I stand at the door and knock; If anyone hears My voice and opens the door, I will come in to him and will dine with him, and he with Me."* The door represents the entrance to every heart. Jesus is patiently waiting to be invited into our lives. He desires to have a close personal relationship with us. This divine relationship is one of peace and protection giving a sense of complete fulfilment and joy beyond expectations that no human being can give.

The offer of God's unfailing love is extended to everyone who seeks Him. We do have the assurance that God is faithful and *"lavishes His unfailing love on those who love Him and obey His commands."*[53] Note the conditional "obedience," which is not to the letter but in the spirit and is a natural phenomenon, coming from loving God.

God is love. When we welcome His love to flow through us, the divine love enables us to love one another naturally.[54]

Prayer is not some fixed liturgy but communication with

God at every level of our lives. We see this clearly in the story of Ruth, particularly the fact that prayer preceded and followed every action undertaken by Naomi and Boaz and Ruth. Their close relationship to El Shaddai determined their life, from utter desolation to one of abundant blessings.

Peter urges believers not to be drawn into the ways of worldly pleasures, such as immorality or idolatry, but to be sensible and to disregard worldly opinions by being

"earnest and disciplined in your prayers. Most important of all, continue to show deep love for each other, for love covers a multitude of sins. Cheerfully share your home with those who need a meal or a place to stay."[55]

The previous passage underscores the demand for prayer, love, obedience and caring for one another—even strangers! These traits, exhibited by Naomi, Ruth and Boaz, were key in releasing God's blessings that turned the impossible to become more than possible! We have a faithful God who acts amongst us today as He did in the past. God does intervene even in the bleakest of times.

Likewise, in the face of adversity, we should not attempt to work in our own strength or mindset; rather, we should have enough faith to trust God, who in His unfailing love will come to our rescue. Adversity or tragic circumstances can often be life-changing for the better. It is human nature when all else fails to turn to God for help. Even a simple cry of "O God, help me" will receive a heavenly response! Humankind was created to have fellowship with El Shaddai.[56]

God is more than able to turn tragedy into spiritual growth and abundant blessings! Nothing is impossible with God. The earthly trials we encounter are a form of discipline that builds character. Though unpleasant for a time, the end result not only builds our spiritual muscles, but also yields an inner peace and joy that money cannot buy.

The discipline is not a form of punishment inasmuch as God deliberately wants to hurt. Rather, His correction strengthens and matures. God is able to turn every trial for our good and blessings follow. Jesus said when teaching about prayer requests that whoever asks will receive, and He draws on the analogy of a father's provision for a child: *"Which of you fathers, if your son asks for a fish, will give him a snake instead? Or if he asks for an egg will give him a scorpion?"*[57]

Historically, time and time again, famine, be it physical or spiritual, follows rebellion or disobedience. God had given specific instructions throughout the ages to live in obedience to His commandments. The early church received specific instructions on how to lead a righteous and godly life, and these instructions are no different from that which was given to the patriarchs and is still applicable to believers today.[58]

In this day, to comprehend how catastrophic a famine can be is fairly difficult. Perhaps it would be helpful to give examples of some of the causes and effects of famine in the more recent past.

Ireland was an agricultural nation with a population of eight million people. Potatoes, being rich in protein, carbohydrates and vitamins, were the staple diet of Ireland. More than

three million people, particularly the poor, depended on potatoes for their nutrition. In the nineteenth century from 1845
to 1851, Ireland experienced a famine that came to be known
generally as the "Great Irish Potato Famine."

The famine was caused by an airborne fungus identified as
phytophthora infestans, believed to have been transported in
the holds of ships arriving in England from North America.
The windborne fungal spores settled on the leaves of healthy
potato plants in the countryside around Dublin. The spores destroyed the potatoes, causing them to blacken, wither and emit
a nauseous stench.[59]

As a result of the famine, the population dropped by two
million. One million perished because of starvation and diseases associated with the famine, and the other million emi-
grated to North America and England.[60] Ireland's tragic circumstances could have been avoided if not for the inertia of
the British government at a time when England was the world's
richest nation. Widespread death could have been prevented
had the British government not been callous to the needs of
their ailing neighbour. There were adequate supplies available
to have prevented widespread death.

The ruling classes attributed the famine to divine judgment. Sir Charles Trevelyan, a leading exponent of this provi-
dentialist perspective, described the famine as follows:

"a direct stroke of an all-wise and all-merciful Providence," one which laid bare "the deep and inveterate
root of social evil." The famine, [Trevelyan] declared,

was "the sharp but effectual remedy by which the cure is likely to be effected. ...God grant that the generation to which this great opportunity has been offered may rightly perform its part."[61]

It is untenable to link the divine providence of God to the laxity of the ruling classes. There was more than enough provision in the hands of the government to have prevented what began as an agricultural blight from escalating into such a large-scale famine tantamount to genocide. God has provided in abundance for the world, but idolatry, self-centredness and greed allowed many to languish in poverty and millions to die unnecessarily.

The Bengal famine in 1943 was triggered by a cyclone in October 1942 followed by torrential rain that caused a fungus disease among the rice crops. Japanese occupation in Burma in 1942 cut off the rice supply, resulting in a serious shortage of rice. The famine induced epidemics such as cholera, malaria and smallpox. An estimated three million people died.[62] The famine could have been less severe if adequate food supplies had been provided.

The priority of the British for victory rather than the import of food supplies caused the starvation in Bengal.[63] Starvation was not the sole cause of death; infectious diseases such as typhus, smallpox and cholera were also prevalent. Whilst Sen and others view the famine as the product of "bureaucratic bungling and accompanying market failure."[64] Gráda, an economic historian, is of the opinion that the population decimation was "largely due to the failure of the British authorities, for war-strategic reasons, to make good a genuine food deficit."[65]

God's promise to Abraham was to provide blessings to all earth's families.[66] The promise still holds today. As with many other continents, God has in one way or another given wealth from the earth He created, i.e., rich natural resources such as oil, coal and diamonds. "Why then," we question, "are so many millions struggling with poverty, whilst a few have untold wealth?" Were these natural resources to be distributed not even equally, but fairly, poverty would be totally eradicated.

Fortunately, today much has been learnt from past errors, particularly where there is good and honest government. Wealthy countries, charities such as Oxfam, The Red Cross, churches and private individuals actively assist with and provide disaster relief to avoid famine. Individuals have volunteered to reside in needy countries, using their God-given gifts to alleviate poverty and suffering.

Despite not having luxuries, those who volunteer lead fulfilled joyous lives while serving in somewhat harsh conditions. Many volunteers are in danger of being killed, either for their faith or simply killed by demented individuals. It is well to remember that everything we possess belongs to God; every blessing we receive is to be shared. Sharing the gospel by words is insufficient. How can a person believe in the providence of God when he or she is starving, homeless, facing a crisis or simply lonely?

Whilst the Bible provides spiritual nourishment, believers must think in terms of giving, particularly to those whose present circumstances make returning the favour impossible. At all times we should be participants in ensuring that those around us should never lack food, shelter or fellowship. What does it take to cook a simple meal and lay an extra plate or two on the table?

Elimelech

The name *Elimelech* is akin to that of Abimelech, which could possibly be a titular name given to pharaohs.[67] The name only appears in Ruth and nowhere else in the Old Testament. No one knows the meaning for certain, but the general consensus among scholars is that *Elimelech* means "God is King."[68]

Generally, in the Old Testament names were significant and were given to represent an event or personality related to the child. For instance, Jabez was given his name because his mother was in great pain birthing him.[69] Perez was named because of his breach birth.[70] Rachel, with her last dying breath at childbirth, named her son *Ben-oni* probably to mean "son of my sorrow" to signify the tragic circumstance.[71]

The name *Naomi* could mean either "good" or "pleasant," *Mahlon* could mean either "sterile" or "sickly," and *Chilion* could mean "wasting away." There is a preference to apply "blot out" and "perish" for Mahlon and Chilion respectively by Midrash commentators.[72]

The family belonged to the Ephrathite clan and were from Bethlehem in Judah. *Ephratha* was an ancient name for Bethlehem,[73] and the mention of Judah may have been to distinguish the clan from another village with the same name, that of Ephratha Zebulum.[74] The clan's name may have possibly been derived from Ephrath, the wife of Caleb, whose two descendants settled in Bethlehem.[75] Bethlehem Ephratha was a small clan in Judah.[76] Rachel died on the way to Ephratha.[77]

If Elimelech was a descendant of Ephrath, the reference to established families would place him as being distinguished and in the position of an aristocratic family, normally associated with authority and being a wealthy landowner. When Naomi returned to Bethlehem, there was much excitement, which meant she was well known to the village people rather than an unknown person.

The people were surprised and probably delighted when they asked the question *"Can this be Naomi?"* (1:19). Naomi's transparent and bitter response that she had *"gone away full"* (1:21) rather supports the presumption that the family were well off when they departed from Bethlehem. We may presume that her bitterness could also stem from her reluctance to leave Bethlehem in the first instance. Rightly or wrongly, Naomi was obedient to her husband as the custom demanded.

Elimelech was in a position of leadership, but more so, in carrying God's name as his King, one would wonder why he deserted his people in their time of need. Neusner, in his translation of Ruth Rabbah, writes:

> Elimelech was one of the great men of the town and one who sustained the generation. But when the famine came, he said; "Now all the Israelites are going to come knocking on my door, each with his basket.[78]

It is also believed that Elimelech's choice of sojourning in Moab was to avoid being derided for deserting the poor. Moab was a wealthy country and like-minded in the sense of being mean, evidenced by their failure to provide sustenance to the Israelites when they passed through Moab.[79]

It begs the thought that if placed in a similar position to Elimelech, would we do the same for our family to survive? Or would we ride the storm and support one another? In the cases of famine mentioned in Ireland and Bengal, the people in authority professed Christianity, yet from their lofty positions, they were far removed from the suffering and deprivation of the common people.

Rather than condemn a person's actions for survival, it does serve as a reminder to care for one another, particularly in time of need, even if it means making personal sacrifices. Today the world is in great need. If every professing Christian was to "walk the talk," the world would be a better place.

Disobedience

Elimelech's migration to the forbidden land of Moab was selfish in his search of personal comfort and fear of having to share his wealth. He did what he thought was right and had acted in his own wisdom. In disobedience, he left the very land that Yahweh promised to look after, as long as the inhabitants obeyed His commands and were not enticed into idolatry.[80] The period of the Judges was the failure to keep covenant with God and was perhaps the cause of the famine.

According to Yahweh's commands and promises, it is not

difficult to agree with Block when he states that it does seem that "Elimelech designed his own solution instead of calling on God for mercy and repenting of the sins that plagued the nation during the dark days of the judges."[81] Sadly, Elimelech and his two sons never returned to Bethlehem nor lived long enough to enjoy wealth.

There was no condemnation from the author with regard to Elimelech's migration, which perhaps was intentional in order to provoke the listeners into drawing their own conclusions. However, it does seem he acted in his own strength, particularly on the count of failing to obey God's commandments and abandoning his people in a time of need. In his desire for survival, Elimelech migrated to what was forbidden territory, rather than trusting God to meet his needs.[82]

God called Abraham out of Haran, with specific instructions to cut all family ties. He partially obeyed as Lot his nephew accompanied him. In Canaan God promised him the land, but when famine hit, he departed for Egypt and encountered problems with Pharaoh. He failed to trust God to meet his needs.[83] Isaac was on the way to Egypt during another famine, but the Lord told him not to go, but to trust and depend on Him to more than meet his needs.[84]

Whilst the audience would have easily associated the idea of migration because of famine with their patriarchal ancestors, the concept of human weakness and God's redeeming love and mercy throughout the generations would have spoken to them. This love and mercy is available to all who believe. No matter where we are and what wrong we have done,

God forgives lovingly when we repent; He remembers our sins no more.[85]

Human Frailty

Abram was a man of great faith, but he too at times appeared to be morally weak. When Abram migrated to Egypt with his lovely wife Sarai, he was fearful that the Egyptian men would kill him so Pharaoh could possess Sarai. As a result of his failure to trust the Lord, he lied and said she was his sister. Pharaoh did take Sarah into his household. God rescued Sarah by sending a plague into Pharaoh's household.[86] Abraham and his family were expelled from Egypt and returned to Canaan.

Moreover, by asking his wife to join in the deception, Abram was drawing her into sin that could have resulted in Sarai's being sexually abused, but God delivered her.[87] Saying that Sarai was Abram's half-sister is true since both have the same father, but a half-truth amounts to just as much a lie.

Abraham moved to Gerar and, whilst living there as a foreigner, he told the same lie to Abimelech that he had told to Pharaoh.[88] This second lie occurred shortly before Sarah became pregnant. God graciously intervened on both occasions to keep the purity of His covenant promise, fulfil His plan, and also to protect Sarah from being violated.

Despite Abimelech's not believing in Yahweh, he was ethically not a bad person. Because Abimelech acted with a clear conscience, God protected him from sin. He and his family were blessed, and God opened the wombs of all the women, who hitherto God had caused to be barren.[89]

Similarly, Isaac would tell the same lie regarding his wife Rebekah in the very same area as his father Abraham.[90] With Isaac and the grandsons who follow, the cycles of human behaviour continue, which serve as a warning that even men and women of faith can lapse into sin.

God's compassion and love in the midst of calamity may be seen in the life of the faithful Shunammite woman, whose son Elisha had brought back to life. The Lord through Elisha instructed her to migrate to the land of the Philistines for seven years because the Lord was sending famine to Israel.[91] When she returned, everything she had was fully restored.

There is good and bad in every person, but the crux of faith is to trust and obey and to realise no matter how grave the sin, God readily forgives those who repent. Life is a journey; at one point or another, a person will encounter situations or severe trials. During these trials, we need to trust God to strengthen us and to resolve the issues. It is easy to make wrong choices in the hope of an instant resolution.

Yahweh chose Abraham to bless mankind. Despite his human weaknesses, he was a man of great faith and generosity. The patriarchs possessed the same human weaknesses as we do today. God, in His great love and mercy, is quick to forgive anyone who repents.[92] We need to possess that same unshakeable faith.[93] Faith and trust do not always happen overnight. Like any relationship, they take time to develop.

Abraham gives us an insight that faith and obedience is a process enriched by trials. Despite Abraham's weakness, the Lord did not waver in His promise that through Isaac he would be the father of many nations, albeit it was slightly delayed for twenty-five years until such time as Abraham learnt to trust and obey.[94] Isaac was the promised child, and Ishmael was a child born of the flesh.

Forgiveness is conditional. The biblical requirement for forgiveness is repentance. As John says, we lie if we say we have fellowship with God and continue to sin.

> *"If we claim we have no sin, we are only fooling our-selves and not living in the truth. But if we confess our sins to Him, He is faithful and just to forgive us our sins… If we claim we have not sinned, we are calling God a liar and showing that His word has no place in our hearts."*[95]

Elimelech was fortunate to have the finances to migrate. Did he in any way abandon families who were less fortunate? Could he not have stayed and helped those in need? Ruth 4:3 seems to imply that Elimelech possessed land and coupled with Naomi's declaration in 1:21, *"I went away full and the Lord brought me back empty,"* indicates that Elimelech was by no means destitute.

The call to help the needy seemed to have been ignored, and his indifference to the plight of the people rather paints Elimelech as a self-centred person. Moreover, it does seem that despite his name, he was lacking spiritually. On the other hand, one could argue that uppermost in Elimelech's mind was to ensure he and his family survived. Most people would want the best for their family, but that choice should not be to the detriment of others. Following the dictates of self-interest is a natural instinct.

In direct contrast, it does seem like those who remained in Bethlehem did not all perish, as friends of Naomi were there to greet her. Additionally, Boaz had obviously remained in Bethlehem and had prospered. Boaz would have provided for the needy and worked his land to produce grain. At the time of Naomi's arrival, Boaz's fields were ready for the harvest.

Disobedience comes in many forms and may sometimes lead to physical death. Sin draws a believer away from God and leads to spiritual death—apostasy. There is no such thing as "once saved, always saved" in the sense that a person can go on sinning and believe it is acceptable to God who is holy and calls every believer to be holy.

False preachers, who preach grace but omit the fact that repentance is an absolute necessity, have led many astray. Jesus makes this clear when He said to the adulteress: *"...and from now on sin no more."*[96]

Spiritual death comes when we pursue those things that draw us away from God. Furthermore, we were created to be dependent on and have fellowship with God. However, because of Adam's disobedience, the nature of hostility and rebellion towards God is within every human being. In this day of so-called human rights and liberalism, many, including Christians, are being drawn away from what God has set forth. The nature, character and precepts of God are being ignored in the pursuit of popularity, materialism and sinful acts.[97]

As a result of rebellion against God, instead of being image bearers of God who is loving and merciful, one takes on the image of evil, which is often associated with lust, envy, murder, greed, strife and deceit.[98] The world in general is currently in rebellion. Thinking they are wise in their foolishness, leaders have failed to observe God's plans for humanity. Many have taken on the role of god, and, as a result, we are witnessing political disarray, mass murders, human sacrifice and religious conflict.

Whatever people choose to believe in apart from God is a religion in the sense that their life's pattern is based on their personal beliefs. Thus, religion will govern people's motives. Religiosity is what killed Jesus! Christianity is not a religion; it is a faith that is completely dependent on God. Faith is the firm conviction that all of the promises of God have been and will be fulfilled.[99]

God does not and has not changed from eternity past to the present day. He gave humanity commandments to enable us to reap all HIS promised blessings. To attempt to "change" what the all-knowing (omniscient) God has set before us to "suit modern thinking" is unadulterated rebellion.

When God allows a period of hardship due to humanity's rebellious nature, there is no abandonment on His part; rather, it strengthens faith even more, and blessings will always follow to those who are faithful.[100] God is ever-present in every aspect of life.

Nothing Is Impossible with God

Joseph was sold into slavery by his brothers,[101] sexually abused by a woman and imprisoned. His faith never wavered, and God gave him divine favour. He was respected and eventually raised to the ranks equivalent to that of a prime minister today.[102]

Daniel was another man of unshakable faith. Despite being taken into captivity, Daniel remained strongly rooted in the promises of God. Even with the threat of death, he refused to bow down to other gods, nor was he attracted or side-tracked by the privileges accorded to him as an official of the court. Daniel did not fast as is the common belief; he simply abstained from eating non-kosher food!

Daniel's manner, despite being amongst idolatrous people, would have been one of gentleness and love, so much so that he even gained favour with the chef! Faced with death, Daniel's faith was greatly rewarded; after facing the lions, he was elevated to rule over Babylon.[103] The Lord was with Daniel in the lions' den, and He shut the mouths of the lions. God is the same yesterday, today and tomorrow![104]

God is omnipotent. He demonstrates His power by choosing the weakest to overcome the impossible.[105] Another example is found in the story of Gideon, the weakest in his family, and his clan was the least in Manasseh (Judges 6:11-18). Terrified of the Midianites, Gideon threshed wheat in a cellar instead of an open floor.[106] When God chose Gideon to save Israel, his faith was wavering; he doubted God.

Gideon was of the belief that God had abandoned Israel and asked God in the first instance to prove He was God, which God did in a spectacular manner.[107] Gideon then asked God for proof that he would deliver Israel. Gideon tested God by putting out a fleece twice, and in both instances, God met his request.[108] Putting God to the test is in direct violation of the Mosaic Law, which prohibits humans from testing God.[109] Gideon, aware of the wrongdoing, asked God for forgiveness.

For the battle ahead, Gideon had raised a twenty-two-thousand-strong army, but God reduced the numbers to three hundred lest Israel would boast. The victory was achieved solely by the power of God against the enemy, who were *"as numerous as locusts,"*[110] Gideon and his three hundred men were able to defeat the Midianites, Amalekites and others from the East who had joined forces for the battle in an utterly glorious and dramatic manner as only God can do![111]

Gideon's battle with the enemy is a perfect example of the power of God to do the impossible. Gideon's victory was achieved not in his own weak thinking or strength, rather in faith and submission to God's directives. This very same power is available to anyone—even to those whose faith may be weakened and in doubt when overwhelmed by impossible situations.

Do visit the Hall of Faith in Hebrews 11 as a reminder of the power of God who makes the impossible possible! God gave victory to the patriarchs not because of their flawless characters; they, like many of us, had strengths and weaknesses. God, in His graciousness, strengthened their wavering faith, and they learnt to trust God to do the impossible.

The patriarchs were in much need but did not tell God what He should do; rather, their prayers were answered as directed by God. Whilst we can bring before God our prayer requests, it is imperative we don't direct God as to what He must do.

Submit to God's directives, which may not always make sense or be agreeable to our finite minds, and your prayers will be answered according to His will.

These divine historical events were given that we might be encouraged to stand firm in our faith.[112] God will see us through even the most disastrous or impossible situations, but we need to seek His wisdom and learn to trust Him and not work in our own strength, hoping for instant gratification.[113]

Although there is no record of Ruth's praying within the narrative, there would have been, deep within her, a faith that matched her initial declaration in 1:16. Ruth's acts of *hesedh* clearly mark her faith in action!

Prohibition

The history of Moab reaches back to the time when Sodom was destroyed. Abraham's nephew Lot and his two daughters survived the destruction caused by the rain of burning sulphur that God sent. Lot and his two daughters fled to the mountains and lived in a cave, as he was afraid to stay in Zoar. The daughters decided to commit incest with their father in order to preserve the family line. Out of this incestuous relationship, the elder daughter gave birth to a son, whom she named Moab and the younger daughter a son named Ben-Ammi (Ammon). These two sons were the fathers of the Moabites and Ammonites respectively.[114]

There was a prohibition whereby no Moabites or Ammonites were to be admitted into the congregation. The prohibition was also extended to offspring of a marriage with a

Moabite or an Ammonite to the tenth generation.[115] However, there was no prohibition regarding marriage to a Moabite, although Deuteronomy 7:3 is sometimes cited. The verse refers only to the Amorites and Canaanites and other dwellers in the land.

The prohibition of intermarriage with other religions was because Israel was easily swayed away from God and turned to idolatry. The same issue stands today, but not because God is against interracial marriage; rather, the concerns that may arise from a believer's marrying a non-believer. It is not unusual for Christians married to non-believers to do a "mix" by semi-adopting the beliefs of a spouse or totally abandoning the faith.

Elimelech's move to Moab may be interpreted in the light of the Israelites' general disposition toward the Moabites, caused by several historical events. Firstly, the incestuous conceptions already mentioned, and secondly, the Moabites and Ammonites showed great reluctance to provide sustenance to the Israelites at the end of their long journey.[116] Thirdly, the Moabite women seduced the men of Israel into fornication that led into obscene worship of fertility gods. This excellent example reveals how personal relationships with non-believers can easily influence religious preferences, such as diluting the sovereignty of God.[117]

In fear of the Israelites, Balak, the king of Moab, hired the seer Balaam to curse the Israelites. Balaam, tempted by the possibility of wealth, used witchcraft. For a time, God did allow Balaam to continue in his error for the sole purpose of teaching him how wrong it is to put God's will to the test in hope of personal gain. God even sent a donkey to oppose Balaam! Balak failed in his quest to curse the Israelites.[118]

Often people are drawn away from faith in Christ, having been attracted by promises of false prophets, seers, wealth or even a spouse! Conversions to other religions generally occur when the question of marriage to a non-believer arises and faith is cast aside for what is perceived to be a better lifestyle and financial security. Oftentimes, the relationship leads to embracing certain practices that give credibility to ancient religions.

Ruth's conversion did not occur in order to secure a marriage or wealth. In the time of dire need and at the crossroads of her life, she proclaimed her faith in Yahweh. In the years that she lived with Naomi, Ruth would no doubt have observed not only Naomi's prayer life, but also her role as a wife, mother and mother-in-law. Naomi acted out her faith in Yahweh. In time to come, David sought refuge in Moab for his parents.[119] This decision is not surprising as Ruth and Boaz were the great-grandparents of David!

Joy and Sorrow

Mahlon married Ruth, and Chilion married Orpah; both were women of Moabite origin. Naomi would not have protested the marriages of her two sons, as there were no prohibitions for marriage to Moabite women. The name *Ruth* is generally taken to mean "refresh" or "friend." Orpah's name is generally associated with "neck" or "stiff-necked" derived from Jewish midrashic to mean she turned her back on her mother-in-law.[120]

The two weddings would have been a joyous occasion in a land of plenty for all concerned. There was hope the marriages of the lads would birth sons who would thus perpetuate the family name. Unlike general Western wedding celebrations, the wedding ceremonies would have taken place over several days, and possibly weeks, with the whole village involved from start to finish. The weddings would have been a sweet relief for Naomi, who hitherto was not only in mourning, but probably bore the burden of caring for her sons.

As time passed, despite the loss of her husband, Naomi may have been hopeful that the wombs of her daughters-in-law would open and produce heirs. She would then experience the joy that comes with being a grandmother. Perhaps as the family approached the ten-year mark, their hopes were high in line with stories of the patriarchs.

Abraham and Sarah waited twenty-five years from the time God promised that they would conceive.[121] Abraham's son Isaac prayed fervently for twenty years before Rebekah gave birth to the twins Esau and Jacob.[122] Year after year Hannah prayed to have a child, and the Lord eventually blessed her with Samuel.[123] Notable in all these instances, each of these long-awaited sons played a part in the history of redemption.

Ten years into marriage, tragedy strikes again! Both Mahlon and Chilion died with no progeny to perpetuate the family name.[124] How tragic and painful it must have been for Naomi, Orpah and Ruth. We really do not know what the three widows felt in their bereavement, but we do know that in the midst of this tragic situation God was ever-present, guiding them into safety, security and fulfilment beyond their comprehension. Yahweh included the two faithful widows in His grand scheme of redemption.

Death Is Powerless

Death is not the "final" word—the "night" may be dark, but *"joy comes in the morning."*[125] God, in His great love, does give strength in times of trial, and it is well to remember that morning always follows darkness. Seeing clearly through tear-filled eyes and a broken heart is difficult, but a time does come when our sufferings become tools of comfort for others.[126]

The loss of a loved one can often result in hurt so deep as to cause both physical and spiritual damage to self and even to family or close friends. Memories are to be treasured, and missing a loved one is absolutely normal, but to enshrine the great loss and sorrow as part of daily life is, in many ways, depriving oneself of peace, which is exactly what the devil seeks to do.

No two persons feel the same when hit by the death of a loved one. We can but empathise, and the only comfort we can give to those who are grieving is to be there, and when possible, speak words of comfort.[127] For believers, death is not the end, but the beginning of eternal life.[128] Losing a loved one is life-changing and being able to move forward can be the beginning of a journey for the better.

The sudden death of a loved one, particularly in the prime of life, is devastating. It is a feeling of indescribable and unspeakable shock, horror, confusion and disbelief. Prayer brings

to the forefront the promises of God who will supernaturally comfort and give an inner peace. How does a person pray
when there is no grasp of the promises of God? While in the
depths of despair, grasping or even understanding the words of
comfort spoken by a priest or those around us is difficult.

I know this to be true as it more or less describes what I
felt when I lost my son. Family and friends surrounded me for
a day or two (some professing to be Christians), but not one
person offered me the consolation of divine Truth. I felt very
much alone physically, but the grace and love of God held me
together in the storm. I shall not go into details as the story is
not about me. It is about how God rescues!

I was a nominal Christian at the time of the tragedy, attending church on a Sunday, wrestling with work and family life
in what seemed to be an endless struggle. The spirit of fear—
the fear of losing loved ones or a monetary loss was crippling
me. I realised my fear was placing me into severe bondage and
stretching to touch the rest of my family. At this time, I relent-
lessly pursued God and found peace and healing.

Moving Forward

Long before The Alpha Course[129] went global, the program
was being offered at my local church. I was reluctant to attend until the day the vicar touched on the subject of dying. A chord was
struck within me when he posed the question: "Are you ready to
meet with God?" Needless to say, I was not! Over the weeks during the course, I began to dispel my belief that God was fearsome
and distant and the Holy Ghost a kind of "good ghost"—but not

a necessity in my life! I knew Jesus died for me, but mine was all head knowledge as opposed to heart knowledge.

At the end of the course, my spiritual eyes were opened to biblical truths, and I began to read the Bible, which came alive for me. My ignorance and fear of the Holy Ghost was dispelled, I was filled with the Holy Spirit, and truly the term *born again* applied to me! It was life-changing, but not an instant total change in the sense that with each passing day, I began to process what it means to lead a Spirit-filled life.[130] It was the trigger that sparked my personal relationship with Jesus, spiritual growth, discipleship and to be what I am today. Fellowship with believers who are lifelong, loving and trustworthy friends was critical then and still is today.

My daily nocturnal shock awakening for some two years at precisely 3:30 a.m. ceased totally, and into the bin went the tranquilisers. Three-thirty in the morning was the time when I had received the tragic news. In time, I discovered that in the three hours I spent alone before dawn trying to assimilate the dreadful news, I was, in fact, not alone! Throughout those early hours of the morning, our Lord Jesus gave me an inner peace and strength to deal with the events that followed.

This is not to say that life suddenly became a bed of roses. I faced several challenges and obstacles in the years ahead. But with each obstacle and challenge, I grew stronger in my faith and learnt that my relationship with God was one of interdependency. We need God and He needs us, His image bearers, to love and care for one another. There is no promise that believing in Christ will avert suffering.

The popular quote by Donald Barnhouse succinctly addresses a faith that grows with time: "Faith is not a mushroom that grows overnight in damp soil; it is an oak tree that grows for a thousand years under the blast of the wind and rain."[131]

Time and again during the years of my ministry, I have encountered several people who have been severely restricted from having the fullness of life because of the death of a loved one. Whilst grief and sorrow are not to be taken lightly, when same people allowed God into their lives, they have been able to move forward and enjoy life to the full. Death certainly lost its sting! It is not just about when a believer gets eternal life, the promise of abundance is applicable in the here and now.[132]

Stepping Stones

Diana had completed the Alpha Course and had come away wanting to know more. Great was her spiritual thirst particularly as she began to delve into the Bible. In the months that followed, we would meet almost daily in the evenings for prayer, supper, followed by a question-and-answer time with her asking for clarity on biblical truths. Hitherto she had been within an Orthodox environment that was rather confusing, particularly the role of the Holy Spirit, healing and the issue of predestination.

Her mother, a devout Christian, had been quite ill for some time, and Diana was her sole care giver. One particular day Diana went to church to light a candle so her mother would be healed. As she explained, a person would place the lit candle for the dead to the right of the church and to the left for those who needed healing (it could be vice versa as she does not re-call clearly).

Sadly, a couple of days later, her mother died, and to make matters worse, with no one around, she sat with her mother ly-ing in an open coffin for three days awaiting burial. For anyone, let alone a young person, this sitting vigil can be traumatic, and for Diana, it was. Even more deep-seated, she felt responsible for the death of her mother. Diana believed she had mistakenly placed the lit candle on the side for the dead and thus hastened her mother's death. Unable to deal with the mistaken sense of guilt, Diana had rejected the existence of God.

One evening during our discussions on the reality of bibli-cal truths, her "candle mistake" and the lies and condemna-tion of the devil, she suddenly sat upright then jumped out of her chair, exclaiming: "It's gone; it's gone!" What went was the backache she had endured for some ten years despite various therapies. Needless to say, she now has an amazing ministry in healing and praying to set people free.

Diana moved from being a "foreigner" in England, with a fair knowledge of the English language, to managing the fi-nances of a five-billion-pound organisation. Her journey was not without trials. Her faith and trust in Christ grew stead-fastly as troubles increased. She did not pray for wealth, but always for divine guidance in everything she undertook. De-spite her own hardships and personal issues, she opened her small, rented home to women in need and devoted her skills to charitable causes.

Eva had lost her brother in a tragic motor accident. Her

parents were so deeply grieved that they seemed to have forgotten she existed. She turned away from them and became involved with idolatry. Late one evening she came running into a church I happened to be attending, saying she had seen the devil and was really scared. I took her under my care, and within weeks, she was set free.

Her mother came to visit and was distressed that Eva had become a Christian. The relationship between mother and daughter was not healthy, even to the point where her mother objected to her reading the Bible. I advised Eva to respect her mother's wishes and to stop reading the Bible for the five days she was visiting and show her faith by actions of love. Her mother noticed the change in her and lifted the prohibition in two days!

Eva's mother returned within a short period to visit and invited me out to dinner. Both mother and daughter were still in mourning, wearing black. During the course of dinner, the mother announced it was the anniversary of her son's death, and the dinner was for him. This gave me the opportunity to share with them my experience and the fact that she had to get rid of not only the altar in her heart, but the altar she had built for her son at home, which was destroying the whole family.

Today, Eva is happily married and back in her hometown. The altar to her brother is long gone and her mourning clothes discarded. The relationship with her parents is firmly established in love with three beautiful grandchildren for them to delight in. Eva and her husband are pastors in their church with an outreach to save women from prostitution. Death lost its power to steal, kill and destroy this beautiful family. Divine activity, albeit hidden at the time, birthed a new life in Christ for all of them.

New Beginnings

Up to the time when both Mahlon and Chilion died, there was no mention by the narrator of Yahweh or of prayers being invoked. However, this absence does not imply that Yahweh was not a part of Naomi's family life. The book of Esther makes no mention of God, yet throughout, Yahweh's guiding hand may be discerned. Ruth's declaration in verse 16 makes obvious that both she and Orpah would have witnessed Naomi's commitment to her faith in Yahweh.

Following the deaths of the two sons, Naomi, Ruth and Orpah would have lacked protection and would have been stripped of any significance they had as mother and wives respectively. Note the shift of patriarchal identity in verse 3 to *"Elimelech, Naomi's husband,"* whereas in verse 2 Naomi was identified as the wife of Elimelech. Thereon she is simply referred to as Naomi, a woman not subjected to a man in control of her own future.[133]

The words of Trible sum up the desperate situation in which Naomi finds herself:

> From wife to widow, from mother to no-mother, this female is stripped of all identity. The security of husband and children, which a male-dominated culture affords its women, is hers no longer. The definition of

worth, by which it values the female, applies to her no more. The blessings of old age, which it gives through progeny, are there no longer. Stranger in a foreign land, this woman is a victim of death—and of life."[134]

Here the narrator paints a picture of absolute desolation: Naomi was bereft of everything precious, her world shattered as she had "banked" on her sons to provide restoration. However, Yahweh had greater plans than her mind could ever conceive!

Sorrowful beginnings moving forward into a new life and fulfilment affirms Yahweh's divine guidance in the midst of tragedy. The stress of the narrative is not on one of disobedience and death as punishment, but of divine providence, which is implied throughout.[135]

Overcomers

George Frideric Handel's understanding of God's providence is reflected in his writings and music. His faith in Christ became obvious particularly in the latter years of his life. Born in 1985 in Halle, Germany, he was raised as a Lutheran. Handel had an incredible gift of setting Scripture and Scripture-based texts to music. He "would frequently declare the pleasure he felt in setting the Scriptures to music; and how much the contemplating the many sublime passages in the Psalms had contributed to his edification."[136]

In 1712, Handel moved to England, where he wrote his greatest music. As a foreigner, he struggled for many years because of great opposition from English composers, changing monarchs and fickle-minded audiences. The Church of England also opposed him for bringing biblical dramas into secular theatres, but this opposition did not deter him either from his faith or joy. John Newton, composer of the hymn "Amazing Grace" often preached against the "secular" performances of *Messiah*. It is to the "secular" that we need to bring the wonders of a gracious God.

In April 1737, Handel's health began to fail, he lost the use of his right arm and hand,[137] but he accepted his disability with calmness and remained steadfast in his devotion to Christ. To make matters worse he was deeply in debt and seemed certain to be heading to debtor's prison.[138] So bleak was his life that he considered returning to Germany. Instead of looking down at his problems, which in normal circumstances could prove debilitating, Handel looked up even more strongly to Christ.

The providence of God is seen in 1741 when a wealthy friend, Charles Jennen, gave Handel a libretto to set to music.[139] Jennen had compiled the libretto from various passages taken from Scripture.[140] On August 22, in his home at 25 Brook Street, London, Handel worked tirelessly, and within twenty-four days, the libretto and score were completed. He simply named it *Messiah*. An oft-quoted anecdote is that, having completed the "Hallelujah Chorus," Handel declared he had seen all heaven and God Himself.

We can surely surmise Handel was working in the presence and inspiration of God, and he used his God-given gift of music to further God's purpose despite personal disabilities. Handel's actions not only blessed him, but all who listened to

Messiah in the generations following, even to this day. Hardly a person who listens to the music is not stirred spiritually.

So absorbed was Handel in his work that he hardly left his house and often went without meals. A friend who visited Handel found him deeply emotional, and as he struggled to describe his feelings, Handel quoted the words of Paul the apostle *"Whether I was in the body or out of my body when I wrote it I know not."*[141] The words and music is an open door to experience the presence of Jesus Christ the Messiah.

In 1751, more problems beset Handel. He suddenly went blind in his left eye, and within one year, he was totally blind.[142] Despite being blind, Handel performed a series of concerts. Handel's fortunes increased dramatically following the premier of *Messiah* in April 1742. The proceeds from the performance were designated to various charities. The impact of Handel's intimate relationship with Christ led one biographer to say of Messiah: "This great work…has fed the hungry, clothed the naked, fostered the orphan…."[143] Another wrote: "Perhaps the works of no other composer have so largely contributed to the relief of human suffering."[144]

God "visited" Handel when he was in the depths of despair and used Handel to accomplish His purpose. Time and again, opposition, which caused him to be ill, besieged Handel, but each time he rose from his sick bed to fulfil the plans Christ had ordained for him. It was not only the end of personal famine for Handel, but it also freed many from poverty, giving opportunities to the "residents" at Foundling Hospital.[145] Providence is divine intervention in people's lives, but it does require action. Handel composed endlessly for twenty-four days; Ruth gleaned from dusk to dawn in the season of harvest.

Following his last performance of *Messiah*, Handel expressed a fervent desire to die on Good Friday, in the hope "of meeting his Good God, his sweet Lord and Saviour, on the day of His resurrection."[146] Eight days later, on the morning of Saturday, April 14, 1759, Handel departed this earth to meet with his sweet Lord and Saviour Jesus Christ.

Handel is buried at Westminster Abbey. Marking his grave is a sculpture of Handel by Roubiliac holding a scroll on which is written, "I know that my Redeemer liveth."[147] Without a doubt, *Messiah* was a supernatural phenomenon. All who listen to this divinely inspired music are drawn into an intimacy with Christ if not, at the very least, a sense of peace. Indeed, Handel's oratorio *Messiah* was a gift from God.

In the general study of church history, the name of Selina, Countess of Huntingdon, is barely known,[148] despite the fact she devoted her time, home and money for the advancement of the gospel. Handel met with the Countess Selina in the spring of 1759. The countess was devoted to her faith in Christ, and her life was not unlike Handel's in that it was intrinsically woven with tragedy, ill health, the poor and privileged, the secular and the Christian leaders of the eighteenth century Evangelical Awakening.

Theirs was an extraordinary meeting of two generous personalities who knew what it was to suffer and yet continued using their gifts for the good of others. They would have shared their unshakable faith that strengthened them amidst their trials and tribulations. Selina herself suffered from ill health, and although denied the company of her husband and children, God used her to further His kingdom. By the age of fifty-one, she had lost her husband and all of her children, save one.

The countess was extremely wealthy and used both her status and wealth to support numerous dissenting Methodist clergy, such as George Whitefield and brothers John and Charles Wesley, in the midst of tragic disagreements that arose within the church. She allowed her private chapels to be used by itinerant preachers. She was so totally selfless in her cause that, when funds were needed, she sold all of her jewellery. She entertained the elite at dinner parties and had the gospel preached to them; at the same time, she would "visit" her servants downstairs and also have the gospel preached to them.

In 1768, at the age of sixty-one, Selina founded Trevecca College in Wales. Trevecca was renamed Cheshunt in 1792 when the college moved to Hertfordshire. In 1967 the college merged with Westminster College, Cambridge. Unlike Handel, Selina is buried in an unmarked grave at St Helen's Church in Ashby-de-la-Zouch, Leicestershire, which was her family seat. Countess Selina had stipulated that no biography be written of her and that she was to be buried in an unmarked grave so God's name is glorified.[149] Singlehandedly against all odds, Selina not only provided for her generation but also left a legacy that Christians would do well to emulate.[150]

The providence of God goes hand in hand with an individual taking action, no matter what the status or circumstance is. Rather than try and seek a change, we need to journey on in faith and hope, with the assurance, *"that God causes all things to work together for good to those who love God, to those who are called according to his purpose."*[151] Faith is holding fast to the promises of God, which in turn makes hope though unseen, tangible. Faith and hope provide the confidence to move into a blessed future.[152]

Enduring the Trials of Life

James instructs us to look at trials as an opportunity to rejoice.[153] The transliteration for trial in Greek is *peirasmos*[154] and can mean "to be tested, tempted, calamity or afflictions." The term *peirasmos* may also be applied to common difficulties that Christians encounter such as persecution of faith, loss of income or illness.

So why rejoice and not lament? Because in times of trial, we learn to persevere and trust God, which in turn produces a deeper and stronger faith leading to maturity and untold blessings. Most certainly it is a time of testing, but God works through our trials to strengthen our faith and trust in Him. Our helplessness does not strengthen us, but when we abandon self and turn to God, He strengthens us.

When feelings threaten or dark clouds or sorrow is overcoming us, rejoice by looking upwards and praising God with Psalms, hymns or worship songs. The darkness will flee! Paul and Silas were in chains in prison having been severely flogged. At midnight, as they were praying and singing hymns to God, there was a violent earthquake. The jailer trembled with fear and was on his knees before Paul and Silas. Not only were Paul and Silas freed, but the jailer and his entire household were saved.[155]

When my granddaughter was a few months old, her father was carrying her down a rather steep staircase when he slipped. I happened to be at the bottom of the stairs and watched in horror as they came tumbling down. I screamed out the name of the Lord and kept praising Him as I reached out to Hannah. When no sound came from the baby for a long second or two, I kept praising God, and to our utter relief, she cried! She was totally unharmed, and her father sustained minor bruises! Praise God!!

Handel, Countess Selina and Ruth shared a common quality—steadfastness in times of adversity.[156] *Steadfastness (hypomone)* is derived from the combination of *hypo* meaning "under" and the verb *meneo,* meaning "to abide." Together they form *hypomeneo,* an endurance while "abiding under." The action of "abiding under" is not "a defeatist attitude of hopeless acquiescence, but rather an active abiding under the trial with faith in God as one's base."[157]

This spiritual strengthening derived from bearing a heavy weight upon one's shoulders for extended periods of time is akin to a weightlifter in training. Developing muscles requires discipline: the heavier the dumbbells the more developed the muscles. Trials develop our "spiritual" muscles. "Most of us do not seek 'to abide under' suffering when it comes our way. Instead, we seek the swiftest way out, which is a general human response."[158]

The Survivors

At this stage, it is important not to lose sight of the fact that inasmuch as Naomi had lost her two sons, both Ruth and Orpah would also have been in a state of deep sorrow at losing their respective husbands of ten years. The scenario following the double loss was one of three women not knowing what the future held for them. In the natural, for Naomi, hers was a future with no hope at all for the survival of the family name.

Although the narrator omits any description of support for the three widows, the contemporary audience would have taken it for granted as the common practice in their culture. Friends, strangers and relatives would have gathered round for the first few days, but not in the long term. Most certainly, the two young widows would have had friends and relatives in Moab.

As with most bereavements in general, even in today's environment, many would gather to pay their respects particularly on the day of burial. However, in the crucial weeks and months ahead, people soon forget or drift away. When reality sets in for the bereaved during the weeks or months ahead, is, in fact, when the greatest need is for emotional and, if necessary, financial support.

My first experience of Eastern traditions relating to death was at my mother's funeral some fifteen years ago in Singapore. She was a Muslim, and as the custom requires burial to be before sunset, many including myself missed the final farewell. When I arrived in Singapore, I was surprised to see every piece of furniture had been removed from the three living rooms and the floors were completely covered in large expensive-looking silk carpets, which I know my brother does not own—at least not that many!

On enquiring the reason as to how and why, I was informed that the carpets were on "loan" by a family friend who owned a carpet shop. Tradition required all mourners and friends to sit on the floor as equals and in deference to the dead. Fortunately, my mother had requested only three days of mourning to be observed, rather than the forty days as normally observed by Eastern traditions of various religions.

Tradition required her body to be bathed by a Muslim woman (none of us qualified as we are Christians), witnessed by other women. Her body was then laid on several layers of white cloth then covered with spices and the shroud wrapped firmly around her secured with a rope. My mother was not placed in a coffin for her burial. According to Islam, her body was laid to rest on her right side, touching the earth and facing Mecca. The young lady (who I knew as a young child) told me she was terrified at being told to bathe my mother as her skin was so delicate from old age, and it was her first time ever!

Relatives, friends, acquaintances and professionals from all walks of life, young and old arrived that evening to pray, offer their condolences and simply sit on the floor in support. What surprised me was the arrival of some twenty women clothed in white (mourning clothes for Muslims) who I had never seen or heard of prior to the funeral.

Some arrived with large catering-size trays filled with sweet and savoury dishes. After prayers, eulogy and condolences were offered, the evening closed with a feast. The second and third day was a repeat of the first day. Eastern funerals are a community event and not restricted to race or religion, particularly in villages. Singapore was by no means a village, but tradition lives on!

Curiosity got the better of me, and I enquired of these women dressed in white. They told me that although they did not know my mother, they had been informed of her death and part of their ministry was to console and provide. For them the act of giving was a blessing as no reward can come from the dead. They came in full force, as they were aware that we daughters and sons were Christians, and our prayers were not deemed valid. I found their deeds of mercy and compassion touching, irrespective of race, religion or creed.

I digress. Neither my sister nor I are convinced our mother died a Muslim. In the first instance, out of her womb came ten children, and but for two, the rest of us are Christians. As a young child, my mother would sing hymns with me, her favourite one being "There Is a Green Hill Far Away." A few months prior to her massive and eventual fatal stroke, I spent time with her, reminding her of things we had done. As I lay by her side, we spoke of my faith in Jesus (she was pleased), and our last song together was her favourite hymn.

A week or so before her death, as I was praying for the Lord to have mercy on her and for her to have a lucid moment in accepting Christ as her Saviour, I had a deep sense it was a "yes." Unbeknownst to me at the time, at precisely the same day and same hour, in another town some ninety miles away my sister, who is an ordained minister, said the same prayer and received the same assurance! You can imagine our delight when we finally got to compare notes. We know she was saved as she fought death for three years!

Naomi would have certainly observed rites in accordance with Judaism, and the community in Moab would have gathered round the three women giving them support. It is likely that Ruth was still in mourning when she went to glean in the fields. Nevertheless, as much as they would have received temporal comfort from the people, Naomi, Ruth and Orpah's deep hurt and inexplicable confusion must have been, for a time, inconsolable. Naomi's only recourse was to turn to Yahweh, whose promise was and still is never to leave or forsake His people.[159] God shows particular concern for widows, orphans and even aliens! "He executes justice for the fatherless and the widow, and loves the sojourner, giving him food and clothing."[160]

God's compassion for the fatherless and widows may be safely extended beyond bereavement to those who grieve and carry a sense of loss having been abandoned by their husbands. These men traded the loyalty and motherhood of their wife for a "younger model" to fuel their own egos or adulterous nature. Whilst society may shun an ex-wife, brand someone a divorcee, single unmarried mother or a reformed prostitute, God does not.

Jesus did not discriminate against women in terms of their past, age or marital status. Several of Jesus' inner circle of followers were women. Most certainly He would have taught them theological truths and empowered them. Mary Magdalene was possessed by seven demons and was healed when she met with Jesus.[161] She travelled with Jesus and the apostles and was present at His crucifixion and burial, and she was the first person to see the resurrected Jesus.[162]

The longest recorded conversation Jesus had with anyone was the Gentile woman at the well, who had had five husbands and was at the time living with a man who was not her husband.[163] She may have been widowed or divorced five times, or a combination of both. In her life-changing conversation at the well, she became the first evangelist for Jesus.

We are not told the emotional state or need of Jesus' beloved friends, Martha and Mary, whose brother Lazarus Jesus raised from the dead.[164] Several women who Jesus had healed followed and supported His ministry and were present at His crucifixion and burial.[165]

Without a doubt, in one way or another, these single women would have had some form of loss or perhaps a form of isolation and were regarded as second-class citizens. They encountered Jesus and believed. Jesus not only met their needs spiritually, He also treated them with honour and respect, when at the time of His culture, the women were often mistreated. Having made a radical commitment to follow Jesus, they received forgiveness, healing, love and acceptance.

Many oppressed lives were changed to one of fulfilment for the followers of Jesus. We can only imagine the sense of excitement the women experienced as they travelled from place to place learning from Jesus. They would have seen miracles, given generously, served and enjoyed fellowship with Him and His followers.

Today life for us can be equally as exciting as we learn theological truths, serve Jesus, and, in turn, serve the wider community, have fellowship with believers, and, most importantly, take time out from the busy struggles of the day to sit at the feet of Jesus in our quiet times and listen to what He has to say.[166]

Not everyone can take daily time out in busy manic lives juggling work, family, kids, shopping and services that keep you holding on to the phone endlessly (great time to pray!) sorting out overcharges or careless mistakes. It is still possible to communicate with God constantly when on the move or taking time out from contemporary social media platforms such as Facebook, Instagram or Twitter! Turning to God in the humdrum of our daily routine makes things go a lot more smoothly. God stands by, in and before you if you invite Him in.

The Bread of Life

Mired in the pits of desolation, Naomi heard that Yahweh had visited Bethlehem, and the famine was over. Who gave Naomi the message? Certainly, there was no direct divine revelation. Perhaps her "hearing" may have come from someone who had travelled from Bethlehem to Moab, having heard of her plight, to give her the good news. There were no phones, Facebook, Twitter or Sky News at the time; neither did they use smoke signals or drumbeats! Village life is a community where good or bad news travels fast by means of personal engagement—an era long forgotten and sadly detrimental to society today.

Many, and in particular, the elderly now live in isolation, with hardly, if any, personal contact. Today's means of communication is by way of Twitter, WhatsApp and Instagram. Contemporary communication platforms are certainly an excellent way of spreading worthwhile news, but in more ways than one have had devastating effects in destroying lives and are contributory to the many who have failed to find a suitable spouse from the lack of community spirit.

The simple message that Naomi heard by word of mouth was that *"The Lord had visited His people and given them bread."* Naomi believed what she had heard: Yahweh had provided food! No doubt Naomi's focus at the time was sustenance for her physical needs. The Hebrew term for food is *lechem* (especially bread or the grain to make it).[167] The direct intervention of Yahweh is the first of two throughout the entire story and, in this situation, marks the turning point of a tragic situation.

The end of the famine is the first direct intervention by the Lord. Hubbard explains: "Yahweh's 'visit' in direct relation to the narrative, means Yahweh has graciously provided food. The narrator has skilfully used the term *paqad* (visited) to mean more than a brief visit."[168] Paqad is often used to refer to divine activity in the Old Testament and could also mean "to oversee"[169] or "to punish,"[170] and sometimes, as in this narrative, "to bestow blessings."

Similar blessing is seen in Luke 1:68 when Zacharias, filled with the Holy Spirit, prophesied: *"Blessed is the Lord God of Israel, For He has visited and redeemed His people."*[171] Our Lord Jesus is the fulfilment of Zacharias' prophecy. Jesus calls Himself *"the bread of life."*[172] Clearly, Jesus is speaking of His ability to give and sustain life. The life that Jesus speaks of is not in the here and now, but as Koester writes, "It is eternal life not bounded by death."[173] It is imperative that in our daily lives we "feed" on Jesus.

In this particular discourse when the crowds had witnessed the miraculous multiplication of bread and fish, they looked for Jesus to provide physical and material benefit. Jesus cautions them not to labour for material things that perish, but to have faith in Him.[174] Jesus says: *"I am the bread of life. He who comes to me shall never hunger and he who believes in me shall never thirst."*[175]

Despite what were cruel tragic events in her life, Naomi had not lost her faith and hope in Yahweh to rescue her. Hearing and responding to the good news of God's providence was the turning point for Naomi as she began her journey into a new life of abundance—more than she ever expected.

As already mentioned, Naomi did not have knowledge of the Holy Spirit let alone knowledge of Christ. She lived a life of faith in Yahweh and believed in the sovereignty of God over good and evil. Despite Satan's will to steal, kill and destroy, God's purpose can never be thwarted.

In the New Testament era, Jesus the Messiah proclaimed He had come to give life and to give it in abundance.[176] The term *life* is transliterated from the Greek word *Zoe*.[177] A life of abundance is not primarily to be thought of in material terms, but rather of living life in the fullness of God in peace. Jesus came to give us the opportunity so we may experience life as God intended. This life is not one of religiosity and austerity but one of godly freedom in love, joy and peace.

The prophet Amos had the following to say: *"The days are*

coming," declares the Sovereign LORD, *"when I will send a famine through the land—not a famine of food or a thirst for water,
but a famine of hearing the words of the LORD."*[178] The past few
years and more so in the year 2020, we see not only spiritual
"famine" but also plagues, as the world has entered the stage of
rebellion even more so against the Word of God.

Rising Out of the Ashes

Naomi's immediate reaction to what she had heard was to
arise from her bed of utter despair, pack what little she had
and journey on to Bethlehem to receive what she considered
her gift from Yahweh—food! Little did Naomi know that by
responding to what she had heard, Yahweh's divine provision
would go far beyond her wildest imagination.

The term *arose* in this context is a strong verb implying
Naomi forced herself to let go her state of anxiety and sorrow
and move on into the future. The verb *arose (qûm)* is frequently used literally meaning "rising from a prone position." *Arose*
can also be used to indicate "commencement of an action especially of a journey."

On hearing his child was dead, King David *arose* from
where he had lain on the ground for seven days, washed,
anointed himself, changed his clothes and left his house to
worship the Lord. He had a sense of peace following repentance and the assurance he would meet his son in heaven.[179]

Believers need to rise up and away from all thoughts and
actions that are contrary to the Word of God and have hitherto
held many in bondage.[180] The vital response demanded by God

is repentance and faith. It is the Holy Spirit that enables believers to live a life that is pleasing to God.[181]

Nowhere in Scripture is there the promise of a life that is trouble free; on the contrary, Jesus did promise there will be tribulations, but with life in fellowship with Him despite trials there will be peace and a way forward.[182] The peace that Christ offers cannot be bought with any amount of money nor even be given by a fellow human.

Circumstances may not change immediately, but perspectives will change on acceptance of the *Zoe* that Christ offers.[183] He came to bring more of God into our lives that we may live a life of fulfilment—not according to our will but His! Many strive to change circumstances in their own strength, rather than trust God to do the impossible. God speaks to His people in more ways than one, but He is sometimes ignored because we choose to hear only what we desire, hence the common cry of "God is not answering me!"

The Lord appeared to Abraham by the Terebinth trees of Mamre, which are in Hebron in the land God has promised him.[184] The visit was twofold: in the first instance, it was to bless Abraham and Sarah with the promise that at the appointed time in a year, Sarah would give birth to a son.[185] Secondly, the Lord revealed to Abraham that having heard *"the outcry against Sodom and Gomorrah, where the men were exceedingly wicked and sinful,"*[186] God would "visit" the cities to investigate. The result of this particular visit was the destruction of Sodom and Gomorrah.[187] Almighty God is not only a God of blessing, but He is also a God of judgment.[188]

The three men who visited Abraham by the oaks of Mamre were the physical representation of God (Genesis 18:1). Two men carrying the presence of God went on to Sodom and met Lot to warn him of the impending judgement (Genesis 19:1). The common belief is that the man who stayed on with Abraham is a *christophany*—the pre-incarnate Christ.

As Morris writes:

> When God visits, everything depends on the state of affairs He finds. The verb *[paqad]*[189] is a warning against presuming on the holiness of God and a reminder that God delights to bless. On this occasion His visit means the end of famine. The bread now available is regarded as God's gift.[190]

The Lord rescued Naomi. In her darkness, Yahweh shone His light, though to begin with, only a faint glimmer. In her weakness He armed her with strength to face an unknown future. With her faith and trust in Yahweh, Naomi was able to release the tragic events of the past. She moved forward a step at a time to receive God's gift, which in her finite mind was bread!

Prayer and hope would have been her only consolation in the darkest hours of her life. Naomi turned to God, even though at times she may have felt God was angry and had abandoned her.[191]

The Power of Prayer

Prayer, as in communicating with God, is the most powerful weapon we have. Peter was in prison guarded by four squads of soldiers, bound by chains and prison guards blocked the door. Fellow believers were saying earnest prayers for him. All believers are commanded to be intercessors!

Peter's faith was such that even though he would be beheaded that very night, he slept soundly. So deep was his sleep that he thought he had a vision of his chains falling off when an angel touched him, commanding him to get dressed and to move quickly. He only came to his senses when he was out in the street! Had Peter not responded to the call, he would surely have been killed.[192]

Where do you stand when it comes to prayer? Prayer enables us to develop a close relationship with God. Furthermore, it takes us away from indulging in self and materialistic distractions that are often the cause of an unfulfilled life. He is our divine Heavenly Father whose love for us has no measure.

Whilst it is good to set aside time to pray, it is even more powerful for our daily lives to include God as often as we can throughout the day in all that we do and say. Take some of the time spent on Twitter or surfing the web for answers or companionship to spend time talking to God to meet your needs. You will be pleasantly surprised at the results!

Throughout the story of Ruth, God is mentioned at the critical turns in the form of intercessory prayer and blessings. The protagonists act and react under this divine covering, the basis of which is faith, a close companion of trust and patience.

We will all suffer in one way or another in life. God is not the cause of suffering. We live in a fallen and broken world caused by Adam and Eve when they rebelled against God in the garden of Eden.[193] God does not suffer with us nor does He abandon us. God is ever-present and active in our daily lives. He is our refuge and strength, and it is into His arms we run and shelter. God loves us and is compassionate and slow to anger. When stress and pain prevail, He can turn our sorrows to joy and peace in His time and way. The end result is a sense of peace and healing, if not physical most certainly spiritual and emotional.[194]

God has a great plan for each one of us way beyond our finite expectations, but we need to let go of what we think is right and stop telling God what He ought to do. When God created us, it was not His intention to cause us harm or even send us to hell. God is relational and desires humankind to have a relationship with Him. Most certainly God foreknew what each person would do in life, and evermore He has provided ways and means for those who have lost their way to return to the fold.

God the Creator has not abandoned humanity. On the contrary, some of those He created have chosen to walk according to their own thinking. In His great love for us, God gave us the freedom of choice. The choices we make determine the outcome of our lives and that of others.

Faith is to trust God to do it His way and wait patiently and expectantly for God to do the impossible. He does! The waiting period does require action on our part and if we fail or make mistakes God will and is able to turn the situation of 'loss' into blessings and success.

The Epic Walk to Bethlehem

To receive divine providence, and, in this instance, food, Naomi had to make the first move. When Naomi initiated the action of departing from Moab, this same initiative is seen in her later scheme of sending Ruth to the threshing floor,[195] which may be viewed as God's redemptive activity behind her actions. Despite Naomi's seductive plan for Ruth, God used her undesirable scheme to Ruth's advantage!

Responding to what she had heard, Naomi made the decision not only to arise from her depth of despair, but to immediately prepare to journey back to Judah. She set off with Ruth and Orpah. For a time, as they walked the road to Judah in silence, perhaps with each one contemplating her desperate need for *hesedh*. Possibly Ruth and Orpah were concerned about whether or not they would be accepted in Naomi's hometown.

Without a doubt, a loving bond unites the three widows, as is demonstrated in the willingness of Ruth and Orpah to follow Naomi. If the lads' names were anything to go by, Ruth and Orpah would have spent a considerable time nursing their sickly husbands, quite apart from taking care of their widowed elderly mother-in-law. It does give the sense of both Ruth and Orpah being caring daughters-in-law, especially in time of need. Naomi expresses their loving kindness *(hesedh)* in terms of *"May the LORD show kindness to you as you have shown to your dead and me."*[196]

One can just imagine the three forlorn widows carrying their meagre belongings, walking, one on either side of Naomi, from the plains of Moab to the town of Bethlehem some thirty miles away, which would have taken some eight to ten days. The journey was not easy, the road would have been dry and dusty, they would have had to cross the River Jordan, and climb the two thousand-feet elevation into Bethlehem. Unaccompanied by males, the widows took a risk as they could have been ambushed and set upon along the way. At some point of the journey between Moab and Judah, Naomi broke the silence by instructing her daughters-in-law *"each to return to their mother's house."*

Returning to a *"mother's house"* for widows is uncommon in ancient times, as widows or women whose marital status changed generally return to their father's house. Judah instructed Tamar his daughter-in-law to return to her father's house.[197] In contrast, Rebekah did run to her mother's house to break the news that Abraham had sent his servant to look for a wife for Isaac.[198] Mothers would have played a significant role in the preparation of a marriage. Now in the twenty-first century, the Eastern tradition still exists, whereby the daughter returns to her "mother's house" (not necessarily a separate building if the parents are together), but rather that the mother will have a say in the marriage union and will play a very important role in preparations leading to the wedding day.

Widowhood

In certain cultures, widowhood was and still is stigmatised. On the death of a husband, the authority in the household would be passed on to the eldest son as head of the household. In some instances, the widow would be cast out or relegated to a secondary role, being replaced by the daughter-in-law. Even in this day and age, in certain sects of Eastern society, the wearing of white garments marks widowhood, and to the extreme, widows are not permitted to remarry.

When my mother was widowed at the prime age of forty-five, she was almost immediately excluded from State functions and society gatherings, which until then she had attended almost daily with my father. A gutsy woman, with no proper education, she refused to conform to the status of widowhood as was expected.

Instead she pursued a career in midwifery and went on to be a teaching midwife, despite her initial lack of education[199] and was respected by all in the medical profession, including loads of women who only wanted her to deliver their babies! She did not remarry, and my father remained the only man in her life. I still meet with the doctors (now specialists) whom she had trained, and the babies (now adults) that she had delivered.

In certain royal families, widowhood means a stepping down from the throne, moving out of the royal palace and basically fading into obscurity. Aristocracy over the ages has similar practices whereby the eldest son is given the status and major bulk of the inheritance. In today's Western society widows or even divorcees, unless extremely wealthy, seem to be relegated to the lower ranks. Invitations from friends are few and far between and in due course non-existent. Widowhood for Naomi would have meant, at the time, total loss of status and finances.

In the Old Testament, God's view of the widow, the orphan and the poor is singularly different from how humanity views them. God weaved into His covenant with Israel His protection over those who are marginalised: *"You shall not afflict any widow or orphan."*[200] God commands that they be taken care of: *"...the alien, the orphan and the widow who are in your town, shall come and eat and be satisfied, in order that the LORD your God may bless you in all the work of your hand which you do."*[201]

Inasmuch as God entrusted His people Israel to take care of the widow, the orphan and the needy, this commandment applies to all of humanity. The widowed and single women also have a special place in the New Testament. At Jacob's well, Jesus engaged with a Samaritan woman despite her reputation and lowly status as a Samaritan in the eyes of a Jew. Theirs is the longest conversation recorded between Jesus and any person, and He pointedly told her He was the Messiah! Although she was not widowed, she does fall into the category of a single needy "alien."

The Samaritan lady at the well was ostracised and an outcast of society, demonstrated by the fact that she had to draw water at a time when no one was around in the noonday heat. She had been married five times and was, at the time of meeting Jesus, living with a man who was not her husband. Emotionally, the lady was unfulfilled and in desperate need of emotional and spiritual affirmation.

Jesus, as was His usual radical pattern, reached out to her, much to the horror of His prejudiced disciples. The Samaritan woman accepted Jesus' offer of a better life and was profoundly changed but did not stop there. This very woman went to the people in the city and testified about Jesus' being the Messiah. Many Samaritans came to believe and invited Jesus to stay with them, which He did. She was the first woman evangelist![202]

Widows were honoured in the early church. The first Christian martyr Stephen and six others were specially chosen to meet the needs of the early church at a time when the widows were being overlooked.[203] A group of widows in Joppa were involved in ministry, and amongst them was a woman named Dorcas whom Peter raised from the dead.[204] The apostle Paul commands us to honour widows and commends the younger ones to remarry.[205]

Poignant is the scene at Calvary when Jesus, in the midst of His suffering, looked down from the Cross in love and compassion for His widowed mother.[206] In His humanity, beaten and bruised, abused and stripped of His garments, hanging naked from the Cross, and shortly before *"He bowed His head and gave up His spirit,"*[207] Jesus places Mary under the care and protection of John. *"From that hour the disciple took her into his own household."*[208]

The way I see it, the "needy" indeed include women and men who are single by virtue of the fact that they are not married or those who find themselves, because of unfortunate circumstances, divorced, widowed or single parents struggling to bring up children. People will always surround the wealthy where money and status matters. How often have we heard of the wealthy who have committed suicide or died from a drug overdose? Wealth is unable to provide the much-needed inner peace or, in some instances, genuine friends.

Overcoming Isolation

A single person, living alone, will at times experience a sense of loneliness. The common resolution is to find solace in drugs, alcohol or a bedpartner. When the partner turns out to be hurtful, desperation sets in! I, as with many other singles, have discovered the richness of life in not only grasping the reality of Jesus' promise that He would never leave us nor abandon us,[209] but also to live within a relational community irrespective of religion or culture.

No matter who we are, no matter how strong a faith and trust we may have in God, we need to have fellowship with one another. Cultivating strong friendships with those around us is important. This does not mean embracing wrong beliefs or practices.

The practice of *hesedh* within our communities and further afield solves the problem of feeling alone but brings with it joy and satisfaction not only to self but also to those in need. A singular act of love and compassion can change a hostile environment or even a person's life. From the time we were conceived, God already had plans for each one of us.[210] Unfortunately, it is within our human nature to do as we please, having been given freedom of choice.

It is God's plan to prosper each one of us. God's promises are irrevocable, but for these promises to be fulfilled, we must follow His instructions! Ruth, in perfect obedience, received the blessings God had for her and the end result was prosperity beyond her wildest imagination! Not only were the plans to prosper her, the bigger vision was and still is for the prosperity and salvation of humanity.

Sometimes we do not and cannot see the bigger picture in our lives, particularly when going though troubled situations. God's promise of protection and prosperity may not often align with our vision of what life ought to be. *"Your will be done"*[211] is often expressed as "give me what I want." In other words, "God, You must do according to my will." Only when we learn to fully trust God and live according to His instructions, will we experience the fullness of life, which is peace and joy, something that no amount of wealth can buy!

Naomi's Farewell

In prayer, Naomi introduces one of the key theological terms in the narrative. As already mentioned, *hesehd* cannot be translated into one English word. It encompasses all the divine attributes of God, in the outpouring of His divine acts of loving kindness, compassion, mercy, love and faithfulness upon undeserving humanity. God's providence denotes His grace and mercy, particularly in terms of salvation and redemption. On a human level, *hesedh* should be expressed in much the same manner where a person acts for the benefit of another without the expectation of a reward.

Naomi's farewell blessing over her daughters-in-law, *"The Lord treat you kindly..."*[212] is consistent with Old Testament affirmations, when situations of parting were under adverse circumstances. These prayer petitions to Yahweh, the personal covenant God of Israel, were to invoke *hesedh* for His people in absolutely impossible circumstances.

A similar benediction to Naomi's attempts to conclude

her relationship with Ruth and Orpah is pronounced by the great-grandson of Ruth, King David. Fleeing from his son Absalom's treason, David was not in a position to provide for his supporters and urges Ittai, a Philistine from Gath, and his six hundred men to leave him and concludes his exhortation with these words: *"…may the Lord show you His unfailing love and faithfulness."*[213]

Ittai, a foreigner, had only recently joined King David's army. Having promised to serve King David, he refused to break his commitment and vows. Ittai's response to King David echoes Ruth's oath made to Naomi: *"…by the LORD and your own life that I will go wherever my lord the king goes, no matter what happens—whether it means life or death."*[214]

Invoking God's *hesedh* may also be seen in terms of blessings and divine wisdom. In gratitude to the men of Jabesh-Gilead who kindly buried Saul, David not only prayed God's *hesedh* over them, but he also promised to reward them.[215] Abraham's servant sought God's *hesedh* when looking for a wife for Isaac.[216] God's *hesedh* is available to all mankind; it is free, and all we have to do is ask! Your request will be granted, and it is life-changing!

Naomi knew for certain that her prayer for stability, freedom from sorrow and peace is something that only Yahweh could provide. In invoking Yahweh to grant *hesedh* to the Moabite widows, Naomi does indicate that God's mercy and grace extends beyond the bounds of Israelites. This of course is apparent when we bear in mind the conclusion of this narrative and the culmination of Christ on the cross. In Christ we have obtained a full inheritance and receive full rights as children of God.[217]

Naomi, bereft of everything, was powerless to do Ruth and Orpah hesedh; thus, her only recourse was to invoke Yahweh's *hesedh* upon the young widows. She knew that only Yahweh could do the impossible in turning the lives of these devastated young women into lives of security and peace. In Naomi's mindset, the path to security was marriage!

It was indeed a sad and emotionally charged moment when Naomi instructs her daughters-in-law to return to their mother's homes for what she considered to be a brighter and secure future. Naomi's use of the term "rest" is not a form of relaxation but rather the opportunity to remarry—*"each in the house of her husband."*[218] Having commended them into Yahweh's hand, Naomi seals her prayer with a kiss. This tender gesture breaks the emotional "dam," and a torrent of loud crying overwhelms the young widows.

Bittersweet Parting

With emotions riding high and amidst the tears, Ruth and Orpah insisted on returning to Bethlehem with Naomi. They use the same verb *return* to counteract Naomi's request that they return to Moab, when they declared they were going to *return* to her people instead of their Moabite homes.[219]

The two widows were prepared to sacrifice the familiar for the unknown in their love and loyalty for Naomi. But Naomi could not be persuaded. Perhaps having experienced much pain and sorrow, her faith in Yahweh was shaken, and her finite mind was unable to grasp the magnitude of God's *hesedh* that went beyond the simple provision of food and emotional healing.

Naomi's response to this offer of sacrificial love seemed rather harsh. She was adamant and attempted to drive home her request by posing a couple of questions. Her first question was not to solicit a reply but to make a statement along the lines that they would be better off not following her, but to return to their former homes. Her response does give a sense that perhaps Naomi had no desire for them to live with her in Bethlehem.

Was Naomi ashamed that her daughters-in-law were Moabites and she would be known for her disobedience? Was she afraid of being ostracised by her people? Furthermore, should they not be accepted into her society, they could prove to be a perpetual burden.

Was Naomi being selfish or was she really thinking of the best way forward for her daughters-in-law? The latter would be more in keeping with a caring and godly woman who had nothing more to offer to her loved ones. Sometimes in expressing deep emotions, particularly as a parent who is helpless to provide, the advice may sound harsh and even cruel. We think of the many parents who have had to part with their children for reasons of poverty. Some will carry the pain and guilt throughout life whilst others take comfort that their offspring would be given a better life.

Naomi poses improbable statements in response to Ruth and Orpah's refusal. The first in the form of a question that she was not carrying sons inside of her for them to marry; the second answers her first that she was too old to marry. Then she contradicts herself by saying even if she were able to do so and gave birth to a male, by the time the child was of marriageable age, the young widows would be too old. She then transfers the onus onto them in that they would not be able to contain themselves without any security for some sixteen to nineteen years!

In today's Western culture for a woman to be married in her late thirties or early forties and go on to bear children is not unusual. In Naomi's time, for a woman to be married in her early teens was customary. Presuming that Naomi had married around the age of fifteen, she could have had her two sons by the age of nineteen, and they could in turn have married by the time they were fifteen. Ten years of the lads' childless marriages would place Naomi somewhere in the region of forty-four years of age. By no means was she too old to bear children, as evidenced by her statement: *"even if I had a husband tonight and then gave birth to sons...."*[220]

What is clear is that Naomi considered herself too old to remarry. Perhaps the suffering that she had long endured had made her worn and weary, and she could even have been experiencing the onset of early menopause. Certainly, for a man, the mid-forties was not considered to be of an unmarriageable age. This is apparent when the narrator establishes that Boaz and Naomi are of the same generation. Ruth and Orpah would have been somewhere between twenty-five and thirty years of age when they were widowed.

For Naomi, God had the freedom to inflict judgment or

bring about blessings. In her stance before God, Naomi was acutely aware that Yahweh controlled events. Naomi ends her anguished rhetoric by declaring that Yahweh had inflicted judgment against her. She expressed her bitterness for not being able to provide for her daughters-in-law in terms of: *"The hand of the LORD has gone against me."*[221]

Bush holds the view that Naomi was not engaging in logical argument or giving reason at all.

> Rather this is the anguished, almost angry, cry of a woman overwhelmed by the bitter knowledge that she must return home alone and cannot drag two young women into the hopelessness of her widowed and lonely state.[222]

Choices in Time of Crisis

Despite her faith, Naomi faltered in her mindset and urged Ruth to follow in the footsteps of Orpah—to return to her people and their gods. At this their junction of life, all three women portray a view of Christians at various levels of faith. Naomi, having heard the good news of God's love and provision, took action but doubt may have gotten the better of her.

Perhaps in her reticence to allow the young widows to dwell with her in Bethlehem, she may have been carrying the guilt of disobedience and was afraid of being shunned. In this time of crisis, she had failed to grasp that Yahweh's *hesedh* included forgiveness![223] Ruth remained stoic in faith, but Orpah caved in under the intense pressure and headed back to Moab.

Christians do sometimes struggle with believing that God

is able and will forgive no matter how great a sin. The very essence of Christianity is love and forgiveness. However, forgiveness does require repentance. The concept of forgiveness finds its roots in Christ on the cross, which is central to the Christian faith.[224]

Forgiveness is grounded in God's faithfulness, expressed in forms of love, mercy and justice. Likewise, Christians are commanded to respond by demonstrating these same virtues to one another. Forgiveness, both receiving and giving is the key to healing, liberty and freedom. God does not waver in His promises.

Naomi did have faith in that Yahweh provides, but, at the same time, she believed that Yahweh also punishes. Her faith was certainly tested to the hilt! The brief definition for the Greek term *peirasmos* can mean "being tested, trial, temptation, calamity or afflictions."[225] Instead of remaining steadfast in this her "last leg of trial," Naomi wavered and decided to direct the course of the young widow's life according to her distressed and downcast spirit.

In the face of adversity, we need strength to walk through trials. Self-reliance does not work because there is nothing to draw from. Most certainly godly advice from friends and relations does help, but they are not with us 24/7 nor do we in most instances reveal or express our innermost feelings. But we have a God who knows every hair on our head and longs to see us through, if we invite Him in.[226]

Christians are encouraged not to lose hope, to be patient in times of trials and to keep on praying seeking divine strength and wisdom from God. To be in denial of our suffering is not the way forward. In time of need, be transparent before God and seek godly people for comfort and resolution. Christians are called to represent God in physically providing for those in need.

In response to Naomi's anguished outburst, Orpah, emotionally wrecked and weeping silently, takes her leave and bids Naomi farewell with a kiss. Orpah's kiss may be associated with other permanent farewells. When Jacob and Laban parted, Laban bid a final farewell to his daughters and grandchildren with a kiss and a blessing.[227] When he was fleeing from Saul, David met secretly with Jonathan, and they parted in tearful sorrow with a kiss.[228] At Paul's final visit to the church at Ephesus, the elders wept sorrowfully and kissed him, knowing they would never see him again.[229]

Orpah

Orpah may have acquiesced to Naomi's request in what she perceived as obedience. It is likely that her "return to the past" was easier than trying to argue with her mother-in-law. Orpah may have felt totally rejected and shaken by Naomi's outburst, and to take a leap of faith into the unknown was too heavy a burden for a sorrowing widow to bear. Words spoken carelessly have the power to hurt or even break a person's spirit.[230]

According to Midrashim writings, the very night that Orpah departed from Naomi, a hundred men and a dog raped her. Out of this degenerate gruesome ordeal, it has been said that Orpah gave birth to the Philistine Goliath[231] and the four warriors of Gath.[232] There is no condemnation of Orpah by the narrator. On the contrary Naomi depicted her as a caring and loving person: *"May the LORD deal kindly with you, as you have dealt with the dead and with me."*[233]

One can only surmise or imagine the consequences of her returning to her mother's house. Could she, would she, have carried her faith in Yahweh back to her mother's house and influenced the household and beyond? A blessed thought indeed! It is highly probable Orpah would have shared her ten-year experience of living with a family who worshipped the one and only God. The narrator has skilfully provoked his readers into considering the consequences of making the right choices. The conclusion by many, including scholars, is that Orpah did return to her gods because of the words spoken by Naomi.

Although Scripture often underlines the importance of worshipping God within a community of believers, it is just as important for an individual to worship God alone. Oftentimes Jesus prayed alone in communion with Father God. Our Lord encourages believers to "shut the door and pray in secret." Believers who pray alone are not alone as God is always present! Believers are encouraged to be in fellowship to support one another particularly in times of trouble.[234]

With the current climate and the prohibition for Muslims to convert to Christianity, the worship of our Lord is done in secrecy or alone in one's room in many Muslim countries. Fellowship with Christians could result in being stoned or even the death penalty. Preaching the gospel is not simply about speaking out one's faith, it is the *hesedh* of a believer in action that draws a person to faith. A superficial religious or "bankrupt" believer is the cause of many withdrawing from the church and even God.

I do believe that God is greater than words or directions uttered by human beings. For a decade Orpah lived in a united household that worshipped Yahweh. Nothing was said about her either worshipping or not worshipping Yahweh during the course of the ten years. The likelihood is Orpah would have been involved in the worship of Yahweh; at the very least, she would have observed and absorbed the family unity.

Whilst the *"return to your gods"* may suggest Orpah had abandoned Yahweh for Chemosh,[235] it is difficult to think in terms of God abandoning Orpah to destruction because of her obedience to Naomi. God's grace transcends the finite human mind; limitations must not be assumed regarding Orpah's on-going faith.

In subjecting herself to Naomi's request to return to her mother's house, it may not necessarily mean her return to other gods. We do not know the course of Orpah's journey from this point of departure. However, we do know that Orpah's bonds with Naomi and Ruth are severed, and she fades out of the narrative. That moment must have been a very traumatic for Ruth as she watched her sister-in-law head back to Moab, possibly never to see her again.[236]

One wonders if the family ties to Moab were ever totally broken. The Bible tells us that three generations on, Ruth's great-grandson David appealed to the king of Moab to protect his parents and allow them to stay in Mizpah when he was fleeing from King Saul.[237]

It is not uncommon for a convert to return to a pagan household and in time to see parents and siblings accept Christ as their Lord and Saviour. In certain countries even though the acceptance of Christ may result in death, we learn of entire families turning to Christ, and it is publicly known many have either vanished, been persecuted or murdered because of their newfound faith.

In stark contrast to Orpah's returning to Moab, Ruth clung to Naomi. The expression "to cling" or "to cleave" comes from the Hebrew verb *dabaq*[238] and implies "a bonding or soldering, that of being joined together." The idea of *cleaving* is generally pronounced by a priest in traditional Christian marriages and is drawn from Genesis 2:24: *"Therefore shall a man leave his father and his mother, and shall cleave unto his wife: and they shall be one flesh."*[239] In her oath to Naomi, Ruth expresses her love and utter devotion along similar lines.

Although Ruth had previously spoken in unison with Orpah, she single-mindedly stood her ground and passionately declared her lifelong commitment to Naomi followed by a solemn oath invoking Yahweh as witness to her pledge.

> The first words we hear from Ruth's lips alone are among the most memorable in all Scripture. Few utterances in the Bible match her speech for sheer poetic beauty, and the extraordinary courage and spirituality it expresses.[240]

Ruth begged Naomi to desist from forcing her to return to Moab. She was determined to go with Naomi—no matter where she was headed—for the rest of her life and beyond. In giving her all to Naomi, Ruth was speaking the true language of love. Ruth had every reason not to follow Naomi who had nothing to offer her. However, in the decade of having lived with her mother-in-law, Ruth would have experienced spirituality, family unity and love despite the grief and sorrow endured. Naomi's tragic circumstance did not hinder her faith but was a demonstration to Ruth that her faith transcended her misfortunes.[241]

The Oath

Ruth made a lifelong commitment to embrace fully Naomi's people and her God (Yahweh) without knowing what the future held for her. In the Old Testament era, a person's religion was very much tied up with their national identity. Ruth's choice for a change of ethnic and religious identity both in the horizontal and vertical dimensions made her an Israelite.[242] Likewise, we who are Christians, whom Paul describes as a *"wild olive branch"* have also been given the same covenant blessings that were given to Israel.[243]

Ruth was emphatic in her declaration that even death would not separate her from Naomi. Ruth's desire to be buried with her mother-in-law was consistent with the Israelite burial custom whereby families remained united even after death.

The concept of being *"gathered to one's people"* is seen when Abraham and Isaac were "gathered to his people."[244] Jacob requested that he be buried with his forefathers. When he died, Joseph carried his remains and buried him in the cave of

Machpelah where lay the remains of Abraham, Sarah, Isaac, Rebekah and Leah.[245]

In her commitment to Naomi, Ruth takes on what would have been considered at the time as the masculine role of father and son in caring for her mother-in-law. Ruth outshines Abraham in relation to faith. Abraham was chosen and promised blessings, whereas Ruth chose Yahweh despite what may have seemed a bleak future. Ruth was certainly not governed by logic. Although there is no mention of God, without a doubt Yahweh's grand scheme of salvation was in action! Ruth was obedient to the cause and calling.

In the words of Trible:

> Ruth stands alone; she possesses nothing. No God has called her; no deity has promised her blessing. No human being comes to her aid. She lives and chooses without a support group, and she knows that the fruit of her decision may well be the emptiness of rejection, indeed of death. Consequently, not even Abraham's leap of faith surpasses this decision of Ruth's...Not only has Ruth broken with family, country and faith, but she has also reversed sexual allegiance. A young woman has committed herself to the life of an old woman rather than a search for a husband... One female has chosen another female in a world where life depends upon men. There is no more radical decision in all history of Israel.[246]

The climax of Ruth's declaration to Naomi comes in the form of an oath whereby she calls upon Yahweh as a witness and judge to inflict upon her disasters should she renege on her commitment to Naomi.[247] The oath Ruth made was in fact more than just a commitment to Naomi. Hers was a profession of faith to Yahweh.

God worked through Naomi and her sons to witness the gospel to Ruth. Ruth's spectacular memorable decision stunned Naomi into silence! We can but visualise the widows with their unspoken thoughts churning in their minds facing an unknown future, whose only hope and faith stoically placed in Yahweh's hands as they journeyed in silence into the Judean hills.

Both Ruth and Orpah would have witnessed Naomi and her sons' faith in Yahweh. Yet only Ruth and not Orpah made a confession of faith. This raises the age-old question of why when people hear the same gospel message, some believe while others do not. Scripture does not fully answer the question, but it does reveal that God desires all peoples to be saved and to know of His great love for us.[248] We who believe must continue to spread the good news not merely by worthless words, but by our actions and self-sacrificial love for others.

God in His love gave humankind the freedom of choice. Ruth chose not to return to her Moabite family and a life of comparative luxury. Instead, she chose to pursue the worship of Yahweh and to take care of an "aged" widow who had nothing to offer.

Orpah was persuaded by outward circumstances and acted in what she may have perceived to be obedience to Naomi and to a better life by returning home to her mother. God did not predestine Orpah to perdition; she made a choice, rightly or wrongly at the time.[249] Within the story Orpah fades into obscurity, but perhaps having a good heart, she may in time recall the promises of God and turn her face to Yahweh.[250]

Grace

There may be times in our own lives when wrong choices have been made, but this does not mean God will abandon us. We are told that God is compassionate, full of loving kindness and good to all.[251] It is never too late to repent and ask God for help. Professing to be a Christian for the first thirty-five years of my life, I made many wrong choices, believing in my own strength and that the only way to success was to conform to the expectations of others. Whilst my life was not unpleasant, I not only lacked peace and fulfilment but was also a very self-centred person.

Only when I realised my idolatry and rebellion did I sense God's taking care of me in the little things of everyday life. I can easily say my sins were as scarlet. My life as a follower of Christ was and still is a journey, but with each step I learnt the necessity of repentance and total reliance on God.

Only in my willingness to submit to the Lordship of Christ did I begin to understand and fully embrace God's unrelenting love and care for me. Life is not without problems, but the difference is I don't have to struggle to overcome the storms that hit now and again and again.

If you are in a position of feeling you have made some wrong choices, it's never too late to turn around. Prayer is not a repetition of just standard liturgy to be repeated as a mantra. Prayer is speaking to God from your heart to express how you feel, what you think, your needs and to ask for guidance. God does know all our thoughts and feelings, but like any loving parent, He wants us to communicate with Him, but not because He needs us. He desires to make us understand that He is in control of our lives and able to provide the best for us. Why struggle when God will do?

Heed what God promises:

"Come now, let us reason together," says the LORD, "Though your sins are like scarlet, they shall be as white as snow; though they are red as crimson, they shall be like wool. If you are willing and obedient, you will eat the best of the land."[252]

God Himself in Christ Jesus bestowed His great love and compassion for us when Jesus went to the Cross and shed His precious blood as the sin offering on our behalf that we may be forgiven. The gift of grace is free; the price has been paid—make the choice and be set free! Let go of the "steering wheel" of your life and instead let God guide you, "drive" you into a life of joy and peace.

No matter who or where we are, Jesus invites us to ask and promises that all who ask will receive. Our Lord goes on to say:

"Which of you, if his son asks for bread, will give him a stone? Or if he asks for a fish, will give him a snake? If you then, though you are evil, know how to give good

gifts to your children, how much more will your Father in heaven give good gifts to those who ask Him."[253]

Ruth serves as a reminder that God is not limited to the people of the Covenant; He readily embraces all who call upon Him irrespective of gender, creed, colour, and from the lowest to the highest in society. The church today is filled with people from all levels of society. In a recent church small group meeting, several members from various ethnic backgrounds expressed that despite being welcomed verbally into the congregation, they still encountered covert racial and social discrimination, an issue that many professing Christians need to address. Underneath the skin colour, we are all red!

Partiality is a sin.[254] Paul makes clear in his letter to the Galatians: *"There is neither Jew nor Greek, neither slave nor free, there is neither male nor female; for you are all one in Christ Jesus."*[255]

The In-Laws

In the biblical context when Ruth embraces Naomi's God and people, she was declaring her commitment and faith in Yahweh. Ruth's oath before God to witness the promises she made is not dissimilar to vows made in a traditional Christian marriage. The bride and groom undertake vows in the presence of God, family and friends to be faithful "for richer, for poorer, in sickness and in health, in good times and bad, to love and cherish, to honour and respect…until death do us part." Unfortunately, in generations past and in present times, the oath of parting only at death has been taken lightly. Adultery is one of the primary causes for the breakdown of marriage.

The marriage vows do extend to family members in the sense of "honour and respect,"[256] as family are all part of the "ups and downs" in life. Ruth honoured and respected her mother-in-law. Genesis 2:24 does state *"a man will leave his father and mother."* This verse does not mean the parting of ways with parents; rather, when taken in context, it refers to intimacy at all levels between husband and wife. Their priorities are to one another and to their children.

The story of Ruth sets before a biblical example as to the importance of family unity, which extends beyond the nuclear family to include relatives. In times of crisis, an extended family will provide support.[257] Most certainly, within a marriage a new and different unit emerges, and parents need to step aside, thus allowing the union to blossom. The Bible states the two become one; however, the new family becomes an extension of family roots carried on from past generations to the generations ahead.[258]

Believers need to confront and eliminate the general malaise towards in-laws, one to another. In any family, the mother-in-law/daughter-in-law relationship plays a critical part in establishing peace and harmony within the immediate and extended family environment.

In-laws are often looked upon as interfering dominating tyrants. Generally, the causes of divisions between in-laws are resentment, rivalry, jealously and the need to control. Resentment may arise from ethnic, religious or social status. Rivalry stems from a mother or even a father who is unduly concerned about the welfare of a son or a daughter, jealous of

CRITICAL CHOICE IN TIMES OF CRISIS

being replaced and will constantly dispatch unsolicited critical advice.

Dissension within a family has far-reaching effects. Siblings are forced to take sides, let alone extended family members. Children are affected as they view grandparents from a different perspective. In-laws should encourage and assist (from a distance) a couple to develop their own values. Support for newlyweds or courting couples from parents contributes greatly to stability.

Admittedly, parents are set in their ways, and newlyweds have their own ideas of what married life ought to be. Don't expect a parent-in-law, son- or daughter-in-law to change overnight. We all have the capacity to change our perspective; situations may not change immediately, but in doing *hesedh* to one another, in time peace, love and harmony reigns.

Naomi certainly attempted to direct the lives of her daughters-in-law in a way that may seem to be rather unkindly. In fact, Naomi did what she thought was best for her daughters-in-law. Orpah fades away, having taken Naomi's advice. However, Ruth having a mind of her own accepted what may have been harsh on the part of Naomi. However, Ruth's expression of love and loyalty towards Naomi changed the course of both of their lives. Families need to be united and not divided; where there is love and unity, extraordinary things happen.

In this day, many parents share the view that children in their late teens or early twenties should leave the family home and learn to be independent. By the time the children marry, the independence gained beyond family life, to some degree, alienates the sense of family togetherness. Because of this alien-

THE BOOK OF RUTH | CHAPTER ONE

ation, it is hardly surprising that parents are distanced, and in time of need, the elderly are left to fend for themselves. Sadly, when they are too ill or old, they are sent to care homes to live out the remaining years of their life.

There is nothing more precious than caring for the elderly, particularly in their twilight years. It is not uncommon particularly in Eastern culture or in rural villages for three generations to live together or in the same vicinity. It is indeed a blessing and delight to gather round the dinner table every evening with family and friends at the end of a day to pray and share a meal.

Sons, just as much as daughters, are treasured by parents. It is not unusual to see parents shed a tear or two at weddings. At this time of mixed emotions, the sense of giving away a loved one should also be viewed as the receiving of not only a new family member but also extended family members.

Naomi not only accepted her foreign daughters-in-law into her home but also loved them as her own. This acceptance is apparent in the way they responded and in Naomi's prayer for God to grant them *hesedh* (Ruth 1:8). Furthermore, Ruth was evangelised not by words alone but by the loving actions of her mother-in-law.

The Arrival

One can only imagine the men who were harvesting in the fields were the first to spot Naomi approaching and would have called out to the women in the village. The women in turn called out one to another, leaving behind their chores and rushing out to surround Naomi and Ruth in great excitement.

Naomi seemed to have been oblivious to the warm welcome and instead laments her portion in life. Sheer relief and exhaustion triggered her deeply felt emotions coupled possibly with the embarrassment of bringing home her Moabite daughter-in-law.

The women in exclaiming "Is this Naomi?" were not as such expressing their failure to recognise her, but rather one of delight. Naturally, Naomi would have aged somewhat with time, and the years of grief and poverty would have taken their toll, but not beyond recognition.

Certainly, on arrival she would have been emotionally and physically drained and exhausted having travelled the mountainous rough terrain, whilst still bearing the burden of her bereavement and financial loss. Was Ruth, at this point in time, being snubbed by the women who considered her a foreigner? Note that for the first time Ruth is referred to as a Moabitess.

As Hubbard explains, the question of recognition raised was not directed to Naomi, but rather by the women one to another, and the question voiced was an exclamation of joyous surprise and disbelief that the Naomi they knew years ago had finally returned.[259]

Their unexpected arrival caused much excitement in the village. No doubt the women would have overwhelmed Naomi with questions. Whilst some of the women would have warmly welcomed her back, others may have chastised her for leaving in a time of affliction. The relief of arriving safely and being amongst her kindred caused Naomi to vent her pent-up emotions of more than a decade.

Breakthrough

Naomi pitifully exclaimed that prior to the family's migration to Moab, her life was "full." Her fullness was associated with the financial security provided by her husband and two sons to perpetuate the family name. Naomi felt such bitterness at her loss that she demanded the women call her *Mara* meaning "to be bitter." The depth of her bitterness is reflected in her accusations against God.

Perhaps during the time of her bereavement and subsequent poverty, she had reflected upon the family's failure to support those in need at a time of famine. After all, her situation had been brought about by disobedience and self-centredness when the family had fled Bethlehem. Naomi believed God had the freedom to inflict judgment or bring about blessings.

Naomi's bitterness may also be seen in terms of repentance before God. Added to her utter despair was her inability to provide for the needs of Orpah and Ruth. Her only recourse was to invoke Yahweh's blessings upon her daughters-in-law, by way of providing them husbands and financial security (1:9). Naomi's prayers were certainly answered for Ruth, whose actions of obedience, love and loyalty towards Naomi were significant towards receiving the blessings of God.

Likewise, our profession of the Christian faith requires action very much on the same lines as Ruth. God demands obedience, not as a legalistic obedience or religiosity, but rather one of selfless love, grace and compassion. As James says, faith without action is a dead faith.[260] God commands us to take care of strangers, widows and orphans, and in doing so, we will be blessed and restored both in mind and body.

In her stance before God, Naomi was acutely aware that it is Yahweh who controls events. In 1:13, she had expressed it in terms of *"The hand of the LORD has gone against me."* Yahweh caused her to return to Bethlehem stricken with the loss of her family and means of support. In employing the term "Almighty" *(El Shaddai)*, she is even more bitter because she believed God had afflicted her (1:20-21). Little was she aware, in her tragic circumstances, God had not abandoned her. In time to come, He would bring about blessings far beyond her limited way of thinking (Ruth 4:13).[262]

We live in a broken world; without a doubt at some stage in life, we will go through some form of hardship—either through making bad choices or an act against us by another person or persons. Even if we were to fall into sin, which is rebellion against God, He is merciful and quick to forgive when we repent.[263]

Oftentimes we may feel that God has abandoned us, but this assumption is far from the truth. In rebellion, it is human nature to turn away and push God aside. Naomi may have, for a time past, worked in her own strength and wisdom. In expressing her profound bitterness, she acknowledges the sovereignty of Almighty God *(El Shaddai).*

Daniel Block is of the opinion that although Naomi had faith, hers was a flawed faith. She had failed to see:

"human causation in Israel's famine and in her own trials...She does indeed ascribe sovereignty to God,

but this is a sovereignty without grace, an omnipotent power without compassion, a judicial will without
mercy."[264]

In comparison, Frederic Bush states:

Naomi here does not evidence little faith; rather, with
the freedom of a faith that ascribes full sovereignty to
God, she takes God so seriously that, with Job and Jeremiah (and even Abraham, Gen. 15:2), she resolutely
and openly voices her complaint. With this robust example of the honesty and forthrightness of the OT's
"theology of complaint," our author depicts in sombre
and expressive hues the desolation, despair, and emptiness of the life of a woman "left alone without her two
boys and without her husband" (v. 5) in a world where
life depends upon men.[265]

The problems we encounter in this day and age stem from total disobedience of humankind's failing to acknowledge the
sovereignty of God and worshipping the desires of fallen humanity who have rejected God and have chosen to do what is
right in their own eyes. The inherent nature of disobedience
comes from Adam and Eve and is frequently manifested when
guidelines or disciplines are deliberately broken. Authorities
set these rules for the safety and well-being of self and others.

Going before God and expressing what is in our hearts is
not a sin as God knows our every thought. More so, sharing
these confidences brings us into communion with God. Rather
than shutting Him out especially in our time of need, we need

to invite God into our every situation. By all means, express your heartfelt emotions as Naomi did in prayer, but with a humble attitude before God.

Do not grumble like the Israelites in the wilderness during the Exodus. Their journey to the land of milk and honey as God had planned was to be a matter of days, and yet it took forty years! They failed to recognise the miraculous provisions and promises of God because they were still in "slavery" mode from the past. Believers are not enslaved, rather as children of God we have been set free!

We need to break away from the things or events that have enslaved us in the past as they can greatly influence our future. Breaking the chains of bondage require us to cry out to God in humility for forgiveness, grace, strength to endure, deliverance and wisdom.[266] Don't tell God what to do; rather, let Him lead you into your promised land.

Naomi, in declaring her bitterness before God and the women in the village, was in a manner releasing her deep emotions and regrets within what she considered to be a safe environment. Being transparent and able to share her burden was a blessing. Jesus invites all who are heavy laden to go to Him who is able and more than willing to give you peace in every sense of the word.[267]

Sometimes it is difficult when our faith is on a downward spiral and we are struggling on our own for answers and feel utterly neglected by God. Pride and fear oftentimes prevent us from reaching out for help. Hence, it is so important for a person to have at least someone to turn to for support and sound advice. Small group fellowship is important, although people come for different reasons. Within these small fellowship groups, we can mature in faith and find genuine and lasting friendships.

For Naomi, God had the freedom to inflict judgment or bring about blessings. In her stance before God, Naomi was acutely aware that Yahweh controls events. In 1:13, she expresses that judgment in terms of *"The hand of the LORD has gone against me."* She later expressed her bitterness in terms of Yahweh having caused her return to Bethlehem bereft of everything (1:21). Naomi believed it was God who had afflicted her (1:20-21). The bitterness and grief that Naomi felt is expressed in her desire to be called *Mara*. As opposed to her given name *Naomi* meaning "sweetness or pleasantness," *Mara* means "bitter" in the original Hebrew.

The pattern set before us in Ruth clearly indicates that whatever the cause for suffering, God is in control; and if we allow Him, is able to bring emotional or physical healing and to turn even the most tragic situation into one of blessing. Christians are not promised an easy life, but the promise we can have peace that is beyond our understanding still stands today.[268] In suffering we do not stand alone as we have been given the Holy Spirit to walk us through the storms of life.[269]

In truth, God did not inflict upon Naomi the tragic circumstance. It was the outcome of the choice Elimelech made to abandon the people in his village and move into forbidden territory. Indeed, God was involved, but not lamenting with her; rather, He was moving in unseen ways to bring her comfort.

God, in His endless love and compassion, will not abandon us, but will give us comfort and the strength to endure in times need when we choose to turn to Him.[270]

Sometimes like Naomi and Ruth, the road to comfort and resolution does involve taking risks and travelling over rough terrain with the possibility of being ambushed by bandits. Their hazardous journey would have taken them some seven-to-ten days and required them to cross the River Jordan and climb over two thousand feet to reach Bethlehem. Despite the obstacles, they journeyed on resolutely not knowing what lay ahead, but they had hope and took a leap of faith!

God does direct our lives and longs to give us the best, but as mentioned we have been given the freedom of choice. Making choices in our own strength and in the flesh generally fails us. This is not to say that God will then abandon us! On the contrary, as we turn back to Him recognising our weaknesses, God is quick to forgive. He does bestow us with blessings that will prosper us according to His plans already determined before we were even formed in our mother's womb.[271]

In taking her stance before God, Naomi was finally able to express her anger and frustration. It is a human characteristic to be angry and frustrated. It is not a sin to go before God and pour out from the depths of our being how we feel. In fact, it is a good move and may be considered as a prayer petitioning God for help. Prayer is speaking to God our loving Father from the very depth of our heart. He knows our deepest thoughts and wants us to go before Him as a child would to a loving parent for our benefit.[272]

Following the tragic death of my son, the breakdown of my marriage, the financial difficulties to the point of not having enough money to buy food and having to raise two rather rebellious daughters, it was indeed a very difficult time for me. In my struggles to survive, I did question God and felt He had abandoned me.

Little did I know at the time that God would turn my life around to one of abundance, peace and joy. My "bad" experiences were in many ways a blessing. The stumbling blocks built my spiritual muscles in preparation for a better future. It gave me an insight into suffering and, as a result, enabled me to reach out to others in love and compassion and see their lives turn around for the better, which is my great joy!

Amidst the clamour of excited women with Naomi's releasing her pent-up emotions, Ruth, a foreigner in Bethlehem, seemed to have been ignored. Naomi, in expressing that she had returned empty, simply could not see beyond what she was feeling. In fact, blinded by self-centredness, Naomi failed to see she had the best companion anyone could desire standing right by her!

Naomi's emptiness would soon overflow with God's blessings through Ruth who stood in quiet repose, looking beyond the commotion and crisis to the promises of God. Ruth's loyalty to Naomi can only come from her virtuous nature and is demonstrated by her self-sacrificial acts of obedience, expecting nothing in return.

The Significance of Ruth in Judaism

Naomi and Ruth's arrival in Bethlehem at the *"beginning of the barley harvest"* is particularly significant in Judaism. According to the Gezer calendar, it would have been in late April or early May. In 1908, R. A. S. Macalister found the Gezer calendar during an archaeological excavation at Tell Jezer. The text was written on a limestone tablet measuring 6.7–7.2 x 11.1 cm. It is not possible to precisely date the tablet, and it could be a little before 900 B.C., soon after the death of Solomon.

Experts suggest a young person named Abijah could have written it. The inscription itself is interesting as it gives us an idea of the agricultural year in ancient Palestine.[273] To date, scholars have not been able to agree about certain details of the translation. A translated inscription reads as follows:

August to September to pick the olives,
October to sow the barley,
December and January to sow the wheat,
February to pull the flax,
March to April to harvest the barley,
April to harvest the wheat and to feast,
May and June to prune the vines,
July to pick the fruit of the summer.[274]

There is ambiguity in the term *Shavuot*; it could mean "oaths" or "weeks."[275] It is interesting to note that Solomon Zeitlin emphatically states: "The name *Shavouth* in the Book of Jubilees has not the connotation of "weeks," but means "oaths."[276]

According to the Pentateuch[277] or Torah,[278] *Shavouth* means "weeks" and was to be celebrated seven weeks or on the fiftieth day after the offering of the Omer. *Omer* literally means "counting the sheaves." It is the verbal counting of the 49 days between the Passover and Shavuoth.[279] It is in celebration of the giving of the Torah to the Israelites on Mount Sinai.

The feast has a twofold significance—agricultural and religious. According to the Talmud, *Shavuot* commemorates the giving of the Torah (Ten Commandments) to Moses from God. Moses was commanded by God to observe the festivals, which, according to the Book of Jubilees,[280] occurred on the fifteenth of Sivan,[281] the month in which the Torah was given.[282] It is also a time of thanksgiving and praise for the miraculous provision and protection during the Israelites' forty years in the wilderness.

The origins of *Shavuot* began as a festival to celebrate the start of the Spring harvest, during late May or early June, recognised as the Festival of Weeks or "First-fruits."[283] In the Book of Jubilees it is also known as the "Feast of the Harvest," when the Israelite farmers would bring the first fruit of the harvest to the Temple in Jerusalem.[284]

The offering of first fruits would also include two wheat loaves. During the offering prayers and Psalms would be recited. *Shavuot* was and still is observed as a holy day dedicated to the Lord.[285] It was called *Pentekoste*,[286] meaning "fiftieth" by the Hellenistic Jews to mark the fiftieth day or seven weeks (omer) from the sheaf offering.

In Judaism, the book of Ruth was and still is recited on *Shavuot*. The post-Talmudic tractate *Soferim* states that Ruth was read on the first day of *Shavuot*, but many later traditions read Ruth on the second day of *Shavuot* before the reading of the Torah.[287] Various reasons are offered for the traditional reading of Ruth. Ruth's act of faith and commitment to Judaism is considered analogous to the receiving of the Torah. Ruth was a convert, and, like Ruth, all Israel underwent conversion when they received the Torah on *Shavuot*!

According to David Ibn Yachia, it serves as a reminder that "the Torah was given only through affliction and poverty."[288] Ruth's astounding commitment, particularly to God, has caused the ancient rabbis and more recent commentators to place her alongside of Abraham. Indeed, Ruth's action is even more impressive than that of Abraham, as she had no specific revelation or divine calling from God.

Jesus went to the Temple during *Shavuot*, and the people were impressed by His knowledge. At the time, Jesus' brothers did not believe in Him; they only came to believe following Jesus' resurrection.[289] On the last day of the feast, the priests would bring water from the pool at Siloam to the temple symbolising water supplied from the rock.[290] The priest would recite Isaiah 12:3 during the procession.

It was at this stage that Jesus invited all who thirst, saying: *"If anyone is thirsty, let him come to Me and drink. He who believes in Me, as the Scripture has said, out of his heart will flow rivers of living water."*[291] Jesus was also referring to the outpouring of the Holy Spirit that was to come at Pentecost.[292]

Christians do observe Pentecost, not as a celebration of "first fruits," but to commemorate the time when the Holy Spirit was given to the apostles and followers of Jesus in the Upper Room.[293] Following His death on the cross and as proof of the resurrection, Jesus was on earth for forty days teaching and preparing His followers about the Kingdom of God.[294] Whilst with the apostles, Jesus instructed them to stay in Jerusalem and wait to be baptised by the Holy Spirit.[295]

Based on the biblical calculations, Jesus first appeared to Mary Magdalene two days after His death on the cross. Added to the forty days that Jesus appeared numerous times and following His ascension into Heaven would be forty-two days. The day of Pentecost would have occurred seven days later bring the total number of days to fifty.

The Book of Ruth
Chapter Two

Now Naomi had a relative of her husband's, a worthy man of the clan of Elimelech, whose name was Boaz.

2. And Ruth the Moabitess said to Naomi, "Please let me go to the field and glean among the ears of grain after one in whose sight I may find favour." And she said to her, "Go, my daughter."

3. So she departed and went and gleaned in the field after the reapers; and she happened to come to the portion of the field belonging to Boaz, who was of the family of Elimelech.

4. And behold, Boaz came from Bethlehem and he said to the reapers, "May the Lord be with you." And they said to him, "May the Lord bless you."

5. Then Boaz said to his servant who was in charge of the reapers, "Whose young woman is this?"

6. The servant in charge of the reapers replied, "She is the young Moabite woman who returned with Naomi from the land of Moab."

7. "And she said, 'Please let me glean and gather after the reapers among the sheaves.' Thus she came, and has remained from the morning until now; she has been sitting in the house for a little while."

8. Then Boaz said to Ruth, "Listen carefully, my daughter.

Do not go to glean in another field; furthermore, do not go on from this one, but stay here with my maids.

9. Let your eyes be on the field which they reap, and go after them. Indeed, I have commanded the servants not to touch you. When you are thirsty, go to the water jars and drink from what the servants draw."

10. Then she fell on her face, bowing to the ground, and said to him, "Why have I found favour in your sight that you should take notice of me, since I am a foreigner?"

11. Boaz replied to her, "All that you have done for your mother-in-law after the death of your husband has been fully reported to me, and how you left your father and mother and the land of your birth, and came to a people that you did not previously know.

12. "May the LORD reward your work, and your wages be full from the LORD, the God of Israel, under whose wings you have come to seek refuge."

13. Then she said, "I have found favour in your sight, my lord, for you have comforted me and indeed have spoken kindly to your maidservant, though I am not like one of your maidservants."

14. At mealtime Boaz said to her, "Come here, that you may eat of the bread and dip your piece of bread in the vinegar." So she sat beside the reapers; and he served her roasted grain, and she ate and was satisfied and had some left.

15. When she rose to glean, Boaz commanded his servants, saying, "Let her glean even among the sheaves, and do not insult her.

16. "Also you shall purposely pull for her some grain from the bundles and leave it that she may glean, and do not rebuke her."

17. So she gleaned in the field until evening. Then she beat out what she had gleaned, and it was about an ephah of barley.

18. She took it up and went into the city, and mother-in-law saw what she had gleaned. She also took it out and gave Naomi what she had left after she was satisfied.

19. Her mother-in-law then said to her, "Where did you glean today and where did you work? May he who took notice of you be blessed." So she told her mother-in-law with whom she had worked and said, "The name of the man with whom I worked today is Boaz."

20. Naomi said to her daughter-in-law, "May he be blessed by the Lord, who has not withdrawn his kindness to the living and to the dead." Again Naomi said to her, "The man is our relative, he is one of our closest relatives."

21. Then Ruth the Moabite said, "Furthermore, he said to me, 'You should stay close to my servants until they have finished all my harvest.'"

22. Naomi said to Ruth her daughter-in-law, "It is good, my daughter, that you go out with his maids, so that others do not fall upon you in another field."

23. So she stayed close by the maids of Boaz in order to glean until the end of the barley harvest and the wheat harvest. And she lived with her mother-in-law.[296]

Gleaning Laws

Gleaning was an early form of a welfare system, whereby the destitute were allowed to follow behind the reapers and collect the fallen grain or fruit. According to God's Law in the Old Testament, reapers at the time of harvest were commanded neither to reap along the perimeters of their fields nor to go back to collect what they had inadvertently dropped. These grains and fruit were to be left for the poor and the foreigner to collect.[297]

Leviticus 19:9 states: *"Now when you reap the harvest of your land, you shall not reap to the very corners of your field, nor shall you gather the gleanings of your harvest."*

Deuteronomy 24:19 commands:

> *"When you reap your harvest in your field and have forgotten a sheaf in the field, you shall not go back to get it; it shall be for the alien, for the orphan, and for the widow, in order that the LORD your God may bless you in all the work of your hands."*

In England, gleaning under common law was a right of the poor, right up to the eighteenth century. In villages a church bell would be rung daily to signal the time period in which gleaners could start and end their gleaning. Unfortunately, this much-needed right was eroded, when James Steel, a local landowner, sued a Mary Houghton for trespass, for gleaning on his farmland. Judgment was given in favour of Steel. The verdict of the case is gleaning is not a right of the poor, but a privilege and must not be seen as a legal obligation.[298]

Fortunately, now in the twenty-first century, the idea of

gleaning has been replaced by food banks and various charitable organisations administered by Christian and non-Christian charities in the United Kingdom. Contemporary acts of "gleaning" may be found in various supermarkets in England. Large containers are provided within the store to encourage shoppers to buy a few extras and drop them into the containers on their way out. Several churches have similar facilities. Not only is it an easy way of giving, but it also serves as a reminder of the desperate need of those lacking the bare necessities of life.

Giving and expecting nothing in return is a privilege and blessing. It is not just about giving money or food; it could be giving your precious time in caring for others less fortunate. When we do these acts of love and compassion, we are, in fact, serving God. It brings to mind the words of Jesus that go even further than simply feeding the poor. Jesus said:

> "For I was hungry and you gave me food, I was thirsty and you gave me drink, I was a stranger and you welcomed me, I was naked and you clothed me, I was sick and you visited me, I was in prison and you came to me...Truly I say to you, as you did it to one of the least of these my brothers, you did to me."[299]

Humility in Leadership

Boaz is introduced into the scene as a relative of Naomi's deceased husband Elimelech. The relationship was not simply a throwaway passage but would in time play a crucial role in determining the future of both the widows. Hebrew scholars describe Boaz as a *gibor chayil*, i.e., a "mighty man of valour."[300]

The term may be applied to someone who has fought battles, has strength of mind or spirit, and a wealthy and influential person, who is highly regarded within the community.

Boaz may have even fought in battles as the story is set at a time when Israel was at war with her neighbours. As the story unfolds, we see Boaz's status when he gathers ten elders of the community at the city gate to convene a legal forum. Boaz himself could be considered a judicial judge.[301] Nonetheless, Boaz was a landowner whose personality shines through as a caring and humble man.

It is noteworthy that the very first words uttered by Boaz to his labourers invoked God's blessings. The way he addressed all of his workers as a community and goes even further by assisting in the fields, indicates his humility and provides an insight into his character. As the story unfolds, these characteristics come into play in advancing the perfect will of God in redemptive history. Note further was used twice in the sentence.

Boaz is the perfect role model particularly for people who are in leadership roles. His first move was to acknowledge all who worked for him, not just his foreman. He worked, dined and even slept alongside his workers. He used his position and wealth to bring about justice.

This point is not to say that in the secular or church environment leaders ought to spend the night on the "threshing floor" with fellow workers! But it surely would not go amiss to spend time getting to know and acknowledge the "lower ranks" as they are the very people who make the greatest contribution to any organisation or the general public.

Good leadership shows no favours but delegates responsibility according to individual strengths and collectively builds a successful organisation. In relation to the church, God has given each person a skill for the unity of the body of Christ as a whole. A good leader will recognise and help develop this gifting.[302]

I do believe every human being has been given a particular talent or strength no matter what the circumstance. We often see even the "disabled" exhibit incredible talents and strengths like athletics, the mentally deficient and blind being creative and some with exceptional singing talents even at a young age.

A body is composed of several parts with each part complementing and supporting the other. As the apostle Paul quite rightly said, "What good is *'the whole body if it were an eye, where would be the sense of hearing?'* or *'If the whole body were an ear, where would be the sense of smell?'* " Even if parts of the body seem weaker, they are indispensable and must be equally honoured.[303]

Ruth's Second Choice

It does seem little time had elapsed since the two desolate widows had arrived in Bethlehem to Ruth's decision to go into the fields to glean. Their arrival coincided with the beginning of the barley harvest in early April,[304] which coincides with Passover. This was indeed an extraordinary decision that required courage, as she could have been discriminated against as a foreigner or even subjected to verbal or physical abuse.[305]

Ruth awakened early that eventful morning transformed from being submissive and obedient to a woman of great determination and courage. The strength and courage exhibited earlier on when she chose to follow Naomi was, in this dawn of a new day, more emboldened in her determination to glean. She exhibited the same traits, but for a different purpose in renewed strength.

One of my favourite passages when I am feeling downcast or weary is the healing and uplifting promises found in Isaiah 40:28-41. The prophet speaks of our strength being renewed by simply waiting on God. Nothing is too difficult that God cannot resolve. Ruth waited on Yahweh. Why struggle in our own feeble strength and wisdom most likely doomed to failure when we can take the more peaceful and victorious route by waiting on God? This does not mean simply sitting around waiting for the miraculous! It could be embarking on an unknown, perhaps even tedious journey armed with hope and faith.

When Ruth announced to Naomi her intention to glean, Naomi's short but sweet response was *"Go, my daughter."*[306] Considering hitherto Naomi had spoken rather bitter words and had totally ignored her presence on arrival in Bethlehem, by addressing Ruth as *"my daughter,"* Naomi's love for Ruth broke all barriers. By acknowledging Ruth as her daughter, Naomi finally accepted Ruth into the Israelite clan. As Waltke writes, Naomi "grants her permission to claim that right."[307]

Perhaps Naomi spoke no further because she was aware of the dangers and was too weak emotionally and physically to get into an argument. As a Moabite going into uncharted and opposing territory, Ruth would have also had some sense of trepidation. However, she trusted Yahweh who had instilled in her the strength and courage to face the unknown.[308] Most certainly Naomi's loving acceptance of Ruth as her daughter would have contributed to Ruth's newfound boldness and confidence.

If I may be permitted to read into the text of 2:2, the simple word "go" uttered by Naomi holds a depth of meaning. The Hebrew term for *"go"* is *yalakh*, which means "to proceed or to walk on." This term is often used figuratively in the Scriptures to pursue a life of righteousness. For example; *"to love the LORD thy God, and to walk ever in His ways,"*[309] and *"If you will walk in My ways...then you will also govern My house and also have charge of My courts, and I will grant you free access among these who are standing here."*[310]

Being ambitious and pursuing goals is not a sin; on the contrary, God wants us to succeed and has given us the solutions in His written Word.[311] Oftentimes in the busyness of life, it interferes with our relationship with God. Many get drawn into the dizziness and razzmatazz of a materialistic and secular world. Sin creeps in when we allow material or personal gains to take priority over our lives and are so preoccupied as to neglect communicating with God. Less time spent with God opens the door to being drawn into unhealthy lifestyles.

The "Chance" Meeting

It does seem rather odd for the narrator to use the term *chance* particularly as God controls everything that happens. God is in total control from eternity past to present and the future. With God nothing happens by chance! It was by no means by a stroke of "luck" that Ruth "chanced" or "happened" to find herself in the fields that belonged to Boaz.[312] Divine providence led Ruth into the field owned by Boaz.

Bush refers to "chance" as the code word for "divine."[313] Proverbs 16:33 states: *"The lot is cast into the lap, but its every decision is from the LORD."*[314] The literal translation of the NIV phrase *"as it turned out"* means "her chance (Hebrew *miqreh*) chanced to be (Hebrew *wayyiqer*)."[315] Several scholars have pointed out that the term "chance" or "happened" must be taken as pointing to the opposite impression given, which is to the sovereignty of God.[316]

Hals logically explains the reason why:

> In view of the story's stress on God's providential guiding of the lives of this family, it is surprising to find such a crucial item in the pattern of events which brought Ruth and Boaz together attributed to chance…How can the same writer trace a chain of events whose beginning (1:6) and ending (4:13) are found in God's all-causality, and then describe one of the links in the middle of the chain as accidental? The answer, of course, lies in the subtlety of the writer's style…The labelling of Ruth's meeting with Boaz as "chance" is nothing more than the author's way of saying that no human intent was involved. For Ruth and Boaz it was an accident, but not of God…even the "accidental" is directed by God.[317]

Nothing in life is by chance. Situations good and bad happen by choices that others or we make. God in His sovereignty controls everything that happens in the universe.[318] In His great love for us, God has given us the freedom of choice. We often make mistakes, but God is able and always willing to turn the "bad" for "good."

The prerogative of every human being is to choose between good and evil. Throughout the ages, the purpose of war, be it religious or political, is to generally acquire money and land at the cost of human lives. The general population in war-torn countries did not choose to suffer; governments who are motivated by greed make the decisions for warfare. Covetousness is in direct rebellion to God.[319]

The family walking down the street, mown down by a drunken motorist is not a chance situation, but rather an act of disobedience by the driver. Where then is God who allows this tragedy to happen? Some will say that it is God's will, and He is right there suffering alongside. I tend to disagree. God's will is not to bring about tragic circumstances or to suffer alongside. Most certainly God is present.[320] Rather God will take hold of evil and tragic situations and will bring about change for the better if we learn to trust Him totally. Wilful disobedience on the part of human beings is what brings about tragic circumstances.

God is love, full of mercy and compassion. God is present, but not in helpless suffering, but extending His arms of love and healing, and it is into His arms that we run for comfort. God does and can change circumstances no matter how tragic, and He will bestow more than we can ask or think with our finite minds.

It is well to remember that Satan and his cohorts have their hand on all evil. The devil's mission is to seek, kill and destroy in sharp contrast to Jesus who came that we may not simply have life but life abundantly![321] It is well to bear in mind that the devil is still alive and active in the most subtle of ways, planting thoughts that oppose God's plans for humanity to prosper.

God daily guides believers into taking the right steps. It may be quite the opposite of what an individual may think. Oftentimes I have heard some believers say that God is not answering their specific prayer. They speak of "waiting" for God to hear from Him, but whilst they "wait," no action is taken!

When a solution is suggested, the response is "I will pray about it," and in most instances, one can translate the answer into "It's not what I want." What they are really doing is directing God to do their will. As a result, a line from the Lord's Prayer, "*Your will be done,*" could manipulatively become "Lord, do *my* will."

Unlike Ruth, believers in this day and age and for the past 2,000 years have been given the Holy Spirit to guide on a daily basis, enabling us to live a life of abundance.[322] We have also been given the written Word of God that reveals His moral will directing us on how we should conduct our daily lives and answers to every issue we may encounter. Nothing that happens today is new or has been overlooked by His written Word. Scripture has been given that we may be complete and equipped for every good work.[323]

Oftentimes when I seek to hear from God answers to an issue or need, I do not hear an audible voice or even a sense of what I should do. When no direct answer is received, I am confident enough to know that as long as I base my thinking and choices according to biblical truths, even if it means having to struggle momentarily, the end result is always a blessing. I stand secure that God is my ultimate Guardian and Provider. In life, the choices we make determine our future. The easy way is not usually the best way out of a difficult situation.

A life of abundance does not necessarily mean having loads of money and living a life of luxury. We are all aware that money cannot give health, peace and joy. On the contrary, it can often hurt us or others. Yes, being financially self-sufficient and not having to worry about paying bills is good; even better is having more than enough to be able to help those in need.

Mankind groans for inner peace, and this can be achieved when we learn to practice sacrificial love. Jesus said, *"Give and it will be given to you...."* Whatever you do to and for others the same you will receive, in fact more than you will ever know.[324] God works through the prayers and actions of a person.

The Hidden Hand of God

Foremost in Ruth's mind was to provide sustenance for Naomi, despite adverse circumstances. Although gleaning was part of the written Law of God,[325] either Ruth was ignorant of the Law or simply applying caution when she sought permission to glean.

By her words and actions, Ruth not only demonstrated courage, but humility, simple courtesy and respect to authority. By going into the fields, the harvesters could have rejected her outright or subjected her to physical abuse (Ruth 2:7, 9). Much as she sought favour from the reapers, little did she realise that God's divine favour was upon her![326]

Ruth's extraordinary request to the foreman to allow her to either gather up bundles of grain among the harvesters in the midst of the field or to take her place among the harvesters was indeed a bold request! Her desire to ensure Naomi's well-being propelled her to be bold, whilst at the same time despite her status, she remained calm and collected.

Either the foreman flatly refused her, or he did not have the authority to grant Ruth's request, which was beyond the normal custom. However, the negative response from the foreman did not deter Ruth. She stood her ground and waited patiently for the owner of the field to arrive. As it was the height of the harvest, at some point, the proprietor would have had to come to the fields to check on the harvest. Her determination and patience were rewarded when Boaz arrived.

Upon his arrival Boaz immediately hails his reapers with the traditional form of greeting, which was then a part of everyday life: *"The LORD be with you,"* acknowledging the presence of God. The reaper's response acknowledges that it is God who gives fruitfulness and abundance, particularly at this harvest time. Both the greeting and the reply are ancient, their origins hidden in pre-Christian times.[327]

Various Christian denominations employ a similar phrase at the end of a service or a Mass. The Latin *"Dominus vobiscum"* (The Lord be with you) is followed by the congregation's response of *"Et cum spiritu tuo"* (And with thy spirit). However, in 1978, the Lutherans changed the translation "And with thy spirit" to "And with you also," which is commonly used in churches today.

Ruth's Status

Boaz would have been familiar with all who worked for him and the sight of a strange young woman possibly dressed in ragged mourning garments, standing in his field would have caught his attention and prompted the question: *"Whose woman is this"?* Certainly, wanting to know to whom Ruth belonged was a strange question! Was there a quickening of his spirit, a curiosity not known before? Was it an overwhelming tenderness towards the figure of a determined young woman not wearing traditional Israelite clothes?

Bush explains why his question was not unusual:

> In ancient Israelite society in general, the community to which one belonged—at all levels, family, clan, tribe, nation, village—was central to one's identity and status. To be resident outside that community was to be a "resident alien," without rights and status. In particular, a woman had no independent status and identity in Israel's patriarchal world. She belonged to and lived under the authority of her father when unmarried.[328]

In response, the foreman gave Ruth an excellent report coupled with a lengthy description calling Ruth *"the Moabitess who had returned with Naomi"* and explaining her request to glean. Two key actions are to be noted here that speak into our everyday life.

In the first instance, Ruth, despite her newfound confidence, and as a matter of courtesy, chose to wait patiently for permission to be granted so as to avoid any form of controversy or abuse.[329] Secondly, as a result of her demeanour despite being a foreigner, Ruth received praise from the foreman. Quite a turn from when she first entered Bethlehem and was ignored by the women and Naomi!

We live in a fast-paced stressful environment that sometimes demands instant gratification or answers. In the process of being impatient towards achieving goals, wrong choices or spoken words may occur that cause grief to others as well as self.

Patience is a virtue. Paul in Galatians 5:22-23 lists nine virtues as a fruit of the Holy Spirit: love, joy, peace, kindness, patience, goodness, faithfulness, gentleness and self-control. Ruth certainly exhibited all of these qualities. The nine virtues may be likened to a beautiful wholesome fruit, that all who see it will be attracted or drawn towards its beauty and taste. Possession of these virtues is the key to success and fulfilment in all aspects of life.

Boaz demonstrated "fatherly" concern when he addressed Ruth as *"my daughter."*[330] Naomi had used this same term of endearment when finally accepting Ruth into the family of Israelites. It signalled that Boaz also accepted Ruth and welcomed her into the Israelite community. Without hesitation, he grants Ruth's request but cautions her to glean behind the female harvesters.

By granting Ruth's request, Boaz has raised her almost to the ranks of the hired workers. Furthermore, Boaz extended his protective kindness to Ruth by ordering his hired men not to abuse her and went a step further by commanding the men to draw water for her when she needed to quench her thirst! Most certainly a turn from the norm, as women were generally expected draw water from the well as Rebekah did.[331]

Grace and Favour

Astounded by his generosity, Ruth in all humility prostrated herself before Boaz in gratitude and queried Boaz's motive as to what she had done to deserve so great a reward! Ruth had taken risks but not without expectations of progress in her desire to survive and to provide for Naomi. Ruth's act of self-sacrificial love swiftly brought to fore the answer to her desire of *"finding favour"*[332] in the fields. Ruth's reputation preceded her.

However, it may be said, Naomi had not up to this point been the "ideal" mother-in-law. Boaz's swiftness in accepting Ruth into the Israelite family was because he had heard of her *hesedh* for Naomi. Ruth had sacrificed every bit of her personal security back in Moab to care for a bitter broken woman in a land where she had absolutely no ties. Boaz was moved by Ruth's utter devotion for her mother-in-law.

Uppermost in the mind of Boaz was to ensure Ruth was made welcome and both her needs and those of Naomi were met. He physically did all he could to ensure Ruth would gather enough grain to sustain both Naomi and her. In his prayer for Yahweh to protect and repay Ruth, Boaz was aware of his limitations and felt that what he had to offer was small in comparison to all that Ruth had done for Naomi. Here we note prayer follows action. It was not just about food; it was also a prayer that Ruth would have the kind of life she once had if not more!

Ruth's steadfast love and loyalty found favour not only from the people around her but most importantly with Yahweh. Finding favour before God demands love and faithfulness both to God and to our fellow human beings. Proverbs 3:3-4 states: *"Let not steadfast love and faithfulness forsake you; bind them around your neck; write them on the tablet of your heart. So you will find favour in the sight of God and man."*[333]

Noteworthy is the manner in which Ruth confidently elevated her status from being identified as a Moabitess from the land of Moab (2:5-7) and her self-designated status of a "foreigner" (*nokriya,* 2:10) to that of Boaz's "maidservant" (*sipah,* 2:13) in response to Boaz's prayer for Yahweh to protect and reward her. By her self-made designation as Boaz's maidservant, Ruth offered herself as his slave, and the onus fell on Boaz to care for her.

Boaz blesses not simply by words but through his actions. Faith without action is a dead faith.[334] Boaz's prayer for protection and prosperity over Ruth testifies to his faith. When Boaz prayed that Ruth would find the much deserved refuge under God's mighty wingspan,[335] little did he know at the time that not only would his prayers be swiftly answered, but he would be the answer to the prayers said for Ruth!

The act of giving is the best medicine for body, soul and spirit! The act of giving should not be laced with expectations of receiving. Ruth had nothing to offer Naomi, but what she had was a faith and hope in Yahweh, which she fully embraced.

Despite her tragic circumstance of widowhood and no clear expectations of the future, her one desire was to provide for Naomi. Ruth began with the most menial and perhaps degrading task, which she performed with respect and humility.

Undoubtedly, her hope was to achieve a better quality of life. Ruth gives us an example of the importance of placing our trust in God that we will receive the things hoped for. However, this hope has to be rooted in the Word of God.[336] Faith is being confident in God and a belief in all His promises. God from eternity past to the present has never wavered. For Chrysostom, faith gives reality or substance to things hoped for. He emphasised the importance of leading a Christian life that goes beyond doctrinal belief.

Chrysostom underlines the objective character of Hebrews 11:1 by:

> comparing the nature of faith with the human faculty of eyesight: "Faith, then is the seeing of things not plain, and brings things not seen to the same full resolution as those that are. For since the objects of hope seem to be unsubstantial, faith gives them substantiality *(hypostasis),*[337] or rather, does not give it but is itself their substance *(ousia)."*[338]

Ruth's task, though menial, tiring and perhaps degrading, was done faithfully. What is your attitude when the task you have been given is not up to your true potential or perhaps too menial a job? The task or trial at hand may be all you can do or give for the moment, or it may be that the work God wants you to do is a test of your character that could open up new frontiers. Starting at the bottom gives us an opportunity to look upwards and to move up towards our goals. In the process, we gain experience learnt with a heart of love, respect and humility.

Ruth's life exhibited admirable qualities. She was humble, hard-working, loving, kind, faithful and courageous. These qualities gained for her a good reputation, but only because she displayed them constantly in all areas of her life. Wherever Ruth went or whatever she did, her character remained the same.

One can only imagine how the women in the village would have assessed her, particularly as a Moabitess. If a sense of discrimination was present, Ruth met this by being humble, without being a doormat accepting what was thrown across her path. Rather, with humility and courage, she toiled from a position of love and faith.

Our reputation is formed by the people who watch us at work, in town, socially, at home or even in church. A good reputation comes by consistently living out the qualities you believe in—no matter what group of people or surroundings we are in. Selfishness and self-serving leads to a breakdown of all relationships. Ruth is the perfect example of one who thinks lightly of self.[339] Selfless love is the basis of all relationships and was Ruth's hallmark—a lifestyle that would do us well to develop and emulate.

The cumulative effect of media, arrogant leaders, worldly views and sin has had an effect on many a person's relationship with God and man. God, in the sense that the preference is to listen to a person and keep a distance to God choosing only what is convenient according to a particular lifestyle. The world is in a mess because of selfish ambitions. It is a sorry state of affairs when even leaders have stooped so low as to slander one another.

A particular celebrity or a certain lifestyle is what many seek to emulate, and when the choice made fails, many spiral down into depression. Being our real self is so much easier, as pretensions place an enormous psychological stress on a person's being. Alcohol, promiscuous sex and drug use lead to death. Only by transforming our mindsets can we move forward.

Oftentimes we hear groans and moans about how unhappy a person is in his or her current employment and are in a constant search for a new job. It begs the question as to their ability to handle a tough or uncomfortable situation and to trust God to turn the situation around for the better. Success does not accompany those who seek a leisurely work life.

Would these very same people who move from job to job receive an excellent report from their manager? It is well to look to oneself as to the cause of problems. Last, but not least in today's world, seldom do we hear the name of God invoked in a greeting whether socially or in the workplace, and this applies even to leaders of churches!

As followers of Christ, we must believe that God has already made plans of what we should do and where we should be.[340] Sometimes we fail to see or understand God's agenda for us. For some of us, not unlike me, it was a hazardous journey. Professing to be a Christian, I had failed to read the Bible and lived according to my own secular understanding. God was kept in a box that was only opened on Sundays if at all!

When I look back to the years of my rebellion, I can only thank God for His compassion, love and patience for me. At times life can prove to be difficult and challenging. It could be for that one nasty person at work, church or home that God wants us to show sacrificial love, which could prove to be a turning point. Some of you reading this book may be struggling for one reason or another. Ask God to show you the areas in which you may have failed and seek His guidance. Whilst waiting, swing into action and show *hesedh* to those around you!

We are to be content with how God has made us. Each human being is composed of a unique DNA—different nations, different skin colour, different shapes, different languages, different status, rich and poor. In trying to be other than what God has made us to be is pure envy, which leads to jealousy, brokenness and a critical spirit. Success in life also requires practical qualities such as demonstrated by Ruth not only in her love and loyalty, but also in her readiness to serve God and humankind. God promised we will succeed if we will lead a life of obedience.[341]

Obedience to God extends to our daily living. We should have respect for those we work for and with our colleagues, neighbours, family and friends. We have been given the rules for right living and, as long as we choose to disobey, we contribute to being part of an angry and disobedient people.

Love in action is to be the hallmark of every Christian!

An Invitation to Dine

Boaz more than fulfilled his legal obligations as a landowner in caring for the destitute and particularly, Naomi and Ruth.

What was the attraction to cause Boaz to invite her to lunch at his table? It certainly was not physical!

The narrator does not describe Ruth's external beauty, but rather her filial devotion and love for Naomi and her deceased family. At the point of meeting Boaz, we may gather Ruth was still in mourning clothes and unwashed.[342] What Boaz had heard and saw was a woman devoted to providing for her mother-in-law and prepared to take on the most menial of tasks. Ruth's excellent reputation went before her and what attracted Boaz to Ruth was her inner beauty overflowing with *hesedh*.

On a spiritual level, Boaz's prayer for Yahweh to do *hesedh* for Ruth was swiftly answered. Although Boaz had provided more than was required, for him it was clearly insufficient to repay Ruth for all she had done. His only resort was to invoke Yahweh's hesedh. Being the godly man Boaz was, the invitation to dine was not on the spur of the moment rather, he would have had time to pray and seek Yahweh's wisdom both for Ruth and his workers. It was Yahweh who instigated the move!

The invitation extended to Ruth for lunch was indeed an honour and a very heartwarming welcome for Ruth. Boaz humbly served her roasted grain and even invited her to dip her bread into the wine, possibly from his bowl. Ruth ate to her heart's content, but as she feasted, her thoughts were with Naomi sitting at home with nothing to eat. She unashamedly saved roasted grain for Naomi. She may have had pockets in her garment or if not, she would have tied the grain into a corner of her shawl.

In contemporary terms, the invitation Boaz extended to

Ruth would be equivalent to her joining not only an inner circle of "executives," but also being given a place next to the CEO who served her with the same food he was eating. Not only was she given access to the nearby water cooler or coffee machine, but a person would be on hand to ensure refreshments were readily available for her! Quite an amazing start to a new job!

Selflessness

At our pastorate meetings, each person attending generally brings their usual evening meal to share. However, not everyone manages to contribute for various reasons. Being aware of particular situations, some of us would prepare a nutritious home-cooked meal large enough to feed several people. A gathering of people from all walks of life enjoy a feast of foods from different cultures. Always having more than enough to eat and seeing the leftovers at the end of our prayer meetings being packed and given to those who were in need was an additional blessing.

I recall clearly one evening when several members were unable to attend. Carmen, Cecilia and I decided that we would each bring either bread or small portions of cheese, and some fruit. As we sat down to eat with what we thought was the perfect amount of food, to our surprise, a group of five young American exchange students living in halls, walked into our room.

We were delighted and invited them to partake with the one large baguette, a couple of packets of crackers, a bunch of grapes and cheese. They were hungry both for spiritual and physical food. We were fed spiritually, and they ate well as we did. At the close of our meeting, we packed the leftovers for them to take away. Food for five fed ten, and the students had more than enough for a midnight snack! Over the years, time and again I have witnessed God's miraculous provisions of *more than enough*.

Jesus was at the temple observing the rich, boastful religious scribes who were making a show when placing their donations in the offering box out of their abundance. Along came a poor widow who gave two copper coins (about a penny), which was all she had as an offering. God measures giving not by the size but by the sincerity of heart and selflessness. *"Great will be her reward,"* said Jesus.[343]

Giving goes far beyond fiscal contributions. Jesus calls us to forgive and love our enemies, bless and pray for those who curse and abuse us, and to give without expecting any returns.[344] Jesus promises: *"Give, and it will be given to you. Good measure pressed down, shaken together, running over will be put into your lap. For with the measure you use it will be measured back to you."*[345]

Many years ago, a lady who will remain nameless broke down and told me an uncle had abused her at a young age. The exploitation had continued for several years. In her mid-twenties, she went from one therapist to another. A particular therapist advised her to have sex with different partners. Following his advice made matters even worse.

Briefly, my first reaction having listened to her story was to ask her to forgive her abuser. At that point she said she would not and could not. I invited God into the situation. I then asked her to mouth words of forgiveness even if she did not feel like it.

Silence and tears followed and when she finally spoke, words of forgiveness came in her words: "I heard angels singing!" What she actually heard (or I did) was the singing of worship songs drifting down from the main church. She was immediately set free from her past, gave her life to Christ, and faithfully served God in more ways than one.

Tightly closed fists have no space to receive, but when giving hands are open, much will be added. The joy of sharing what little we may have whether it be in material terms, love to the unloved or by actions of comfort is immeasurable. In the process we witness God's *hesedh* in more ways than one. So much joy is involved in giving not just in terms of material things but in the multiplication of relationships.

Selfishness and self-serving lead to breakdown of all relationships—at home, in the community and in the workplace. Ruth is a perfect example of one who thinks lightly of self. Hers was a deeply committed faith confident in the knowledge that Yahweh would meet her needs. Although she was burdened, she courageously faced the challenge by way of her humility and selflessness. The key to living a life of abundance is in caring for the needs of others before self.

The perfect example set before us is that of Jesus Christ, who despite being God, did not cling to His mighty sovereign status. Instead, He chose to come into this world in all humility in human form to serve and save us. We are called to have the same mindset as Christ.

"Do nothing from selfish ambition or conceit, but in humility count others more significant than yourselves. Let

each of you look not only to [his /her][346] own interests, but also to the interests of others. Have this mind among yourselves, which is yours in Christ Jesus, who, though he was in the form of God, did not count equality with God, a thing to be grasped, but emptied Himself, by taking the form of a servant, being born in the likeness of men. And being found in human form, He humbled Himself by becoming obedient to the point of death, even death on a cross."[347]

Throughout the narrative, Ruth does not pray out loud or at set times or attempt to go before God with a "shopping list"! Her communion with God was one of a close relationship. By close relationship, I mean a constant awareness of His presence, be it in times of joy, stress, sorrow, or illness. This form of prayer helps us through the myriad of our emotions that can sometimes blind us to the power of God where nothing is impossible!

We are encouraged to set aside specific times alone with God. Why not simply extend these times to include God with our every move big and small consistently throughout the day? Seek God's wisdom and blessings on everything, and you will discover the peace and confidence of the continuous presence of God. No doubt whilst Ruth was gleaning, she would have been praising God for the bounty despite the toil.

In the course of the day, particularly when doing what we think is not our "job," instead of reluctance or rebellion, give thanks and praise instead. During stressful times, even in the midst of an argument, stop and ask God to take charge. Even in the most menial of tasks, which do not require much brainwork, joyfully accept and praise God. You will experience not only the peace you seek, but answers to your needs. The choice is yours to make. Choose between discontentment or peace and joy!

A Basketful of Love

We know the stalks were deliberately left by the hired hands for Ruth to pick up. At the end of her day of gleaning, Ruth would beat out the grains from the stalk. I have seen threshing on a small scale in Far East countries. She may have, not unlike what I have seen, beaten the stalks over a piece of wood or a stone boulder, letting the grain fall into a container. Then she would have tossed the grain, using a form of woven tray, into the air for the chaff to be blown away, leaving the clean grain to fall back into the woven tray. She may, of course, have left the chore of cleaning the grain to Naomi!

Women in Ruth's time would have worn long garments and shawls that would drape from their heads down to the ankles. These shawls were most useful as they could be used as head coverings, protection from sandstorms and for keeping warm. A similar form of wearing long garments and shawls (shorter version) is still used by traditional Muslims. In the Far East countries, oftentimes these shawls are used as baby carriers on the backs of mothers who work in the fields. Malays wear shawls known as *selendangs* to cover their heads, keep warm or as a fashion accessory draped over one shoulder.

Scriptures says Ruth gleaned a basketful of grain equivalent to an ephah of barley. Scholars and historians to date have not come to a conclusive agreement of how much Ruth collected in terms of weight. Campbell states at most it could be 47:6 pounds, but more favourable would be Scott's calculation of 29 pounds.[348]

Ruth would have had no basket to carry the grain home. It's likely she would have formed a container by tying the corners of her shawl together to form a pouch and slung this over her shoulders for the journey home. After a long day filled with the unexpected with much to think and thank Yahweh for her bounty, Ruth trundles home into the city with a bagful of surprises for Naomi.

Despite what views you may have about Naomi, like any caring person, she would have been concerned about Ruth's gleaning in an unknown field amongst men who may verbally or even physically abuse her. As dusk sets in and the room darkens, Naomi would have sunk deeper into despair. No lamp, no food and worse still, no Ruth! One can imagine the "what if's?" racing through Naomi's mind.

Into the darkened room walks Ruth with her shawl full of grain! As she carefully lowers her bundle to the floor, she reaches into her pocket for the roasted grain and hands it to Naomi. It would have been an astounding moment for Naomi! Her first reaction was to pray blessings over the unknown benefactor, for hitherto Ruth had not mentioned Boaz.

For Ruth to see her mother-in-law animated by the provision of food must have been such a joy. Indeed, even a jaw-dropping moment for Naomi! The load of grain undoubtedly lifted the heavy emotional load off Naomi, who moved from the depths of depression to acknowledging Yahweh's *hesedh*. She moved from famine to being fed!

The second surprise was even more overwhelming for Naomi when Ruth mentioned the name of Boaz as the owner of the field. This prompted Naomi to pray a second blessing over Boaz for his loving kindness and giving thanks to Yahweh for His faithfulness in caring for Ruth and herself.[349] Naomi moved from a state of hopelessness to one of hope.

Naomi gushes on to explain to Ruth that Boaz was one of a group of relatives who should be responsible for their wellbeing. Up to this point, Ruth would not have known who Boaz was. Boaz certainly demonstrated his generosity on that very first day, but he was not legally bound to redeem either Ruth or Naomi in the sense of marriage.

One can only imagine Naomi's mind racing as to how she could ensnare Boaz for Ruth. Were the thoughts of a possible marriage to Boaz already in her mind? Naomi would have been aware of the customs of inheritance. Perhaps during the weeks of harvesting Naomi would have been planning the ways and means to seek the support of Boaz or even a scheme to ensnare Boaz into marrying Ruth.

Providence

This whole story is about God's providence. Hals calls us to "approach the narrative with the awareness that it deals with the hiddenness of God's acting in human affairs."[350] Whilst many Christians say they hear daily from God, just as many, if not more, say they do not hear anything—not even a whisper! Be encouraged, you who are sometimes disheartened; although you may not hear or even sense what God is saying, be assured that in His "hiddenness," He knows your every need and will never fail you if you lean on Him.

The assurance comes from Jesus Himself when He said in John 14:18 that He would not leave us as orphans. Furthermore, Jesus sent His Holy Spirit to live within us and to guide us through life.[351] God does communicate with us daily at least by way of the Bible. Ruth had neither His Spirit nor His Word, but her faithfulness and obedience to Naomi was a clear reflection of her obedience to Yahweh. So, the call to a life of self-sacrificial love and obedience to God's commands is for us all.

We all have failed one way or another, be it wilfully or simply through careless disobedience. Self-centredness leads to the breakdown of relationships. The inability to love others stems from not loving self, the root of which is the inability to love God with all our hearts and minds. My philosophy in life is to put God first and everything else follows. The eyes of God search the whole earth to strengthen those whose hearts are fully committed to Him.[352]

God used Ruth the Moabitess in the golden chain of His redemptive plans not only for the protagonists, but for all people today. God longs to involve us all in His plans for the redemption of mankind. Throughout redemptive history to the birth of the longed-for Messiah, God used ordinary people just like you and me and sometimes even people we may consider immoral or weak to do great things. Are you willing to be part of the plan to fulfil God's purpose in blessing all nations? The key is obedience!

Ruth sets for us all an example of how situations can change, and it is also an assurance that nothing is impossible with God. Ruth's story began with wealth, moved into tragedy, and closed with fulfilment. According to some Jewish literature, she was the daughter of a king.

Ruth married into what may be considered a family that was very well off. Her husband of ten years was a man of ill health who eventually died, and she was left childless. She became destitute. Should any part of these tragic situation resonate with you, my encouragement is not to give up hope and to draw from Ruth how things can and will change.

In 1996, I was able to purchase a rather dilapidated three-bedroomed garden flat in Chelsea. As far as I was concerned, this was to be my permanent home never to move again. I spent a year renovating the flat turning it into a beautiful home. Little did I realise it was to be the beginning of a long journey of trials and at the same time of God's grace and compassion.

The obstacles I encountered were in fact building blocks to spiritual maturity and advancement. I knew God had a plan, but what it was to be I did not know at the time of my trials. I had to simply trust God as it was beyond mine, or human control as the situation was embedded in greed and lies.

At the time of purchase, I knew it was a leasehold property that was to be renewed in four years. My solicitors assured me the lease could be renewed. The years spent at the flat were a blessing. During this time, I led a home group and felt a strong calling to study theology, which I did.

Midway through my studies, the time came for the lease to be renewed. Unfortunately, the leaseholders were not willing to do so. This unwillingness, of course, resulted in a long, drawn-out, expensive court case. I lost my home due to a legal technicality that my solicitors had overlooked. I was homeless!

Naturally, family, friends and pastors had prayed for victory. The victory came but not according to human desires. Despite the rather stressful time, I carried on as normal with my home group, studying, counselling and helping those in need. The compensation paid was insufficient to purchase another home, but enough to pay the solicitors with a little left over for me to survive.

During this dire period, I prayed but God seemed so silent. I had a sense of peace but also one of bewilderment as to why this had happened. Sadly, prior to the application for renewal of the leasehold, the solicitor who did my conveyance for the flat had died as a result of a boating accident and was not around to admit the failure on the part of his firm.

When the time came for me to leave my home, I packed everything I owned and placed my belongings in storage. All I kept was a suitcase with the only barest essentials. I would not see my belongings for some fourteen years. My final act in the home that had given me joy and peace was to give it a thorough clean and polish. I even left flowers and plants that I had nurtured over the years.

During the days of packing my belongings, although rather sad and very bewildered, I was in no way angry. I prayed and glorified God to those around me who were totally baffled at my attitude. Friends and family, especially those who had fasted and prayed for financial victory, felt that I had been let down by

God. All prayers were heard and answered but in God's time, plans and purpose.

To be honest, I did not fast, but I did ask God to show me what next. Nothing! God seemed to have gone silent on me. I decided to take action. I had recently read Jackie Pullinger's book entitled *Chasing the Dragon* and thought perhaps I should follow her footsteps of "going" into nowhere until such time as God stopped me in the place He wanted me to be.

In the haziness of everything that had transpired, I decided the best way forward was to head for Europe, and when God decided for me to stop, I would. Perhaps God needed me to step out of my comfort zone. The journey would require me to cross Chelsea Bridge and head south to take a ferry to France.

On the first day heading towards the Chelsea Bridge, my sister called and was horrified to hear I was going on a journey to nowhere. She immediately invited me to spend time in her fabulous home. I thought perhaps this was what I had to do whilst waiting to hear what God had to say—nothing! Two days spent with her was very pleasant, but I was restless and decided my calling was somewhere else in the remote hills of Europe.

On the third day, as I was some fifty yards away from Chelsea Bridge, my mobile rang. The call from abroad was a potentate for whom I had done some work over the past years. Though I had expected nothing in return, the family had left me the keys to their home. On hearing of my intentions, I assured them the keys had been left in safe hands, awaiting collection on their arrival in London.

To my utter amazement, I was asked not to proceed further

but to turn around and stay in their home as a temporary solution to gather my thoughts and complete my degree. Was this God's intervening? Yes! His ways are bigger than mine! Twice I was stopped at almost the same point.

The home my benefactors offered me was better than anything I could have dreamt of. Whilst staying at the Residence, I went on to complete a master's degree, set up a charity, run a pastorate and care for those in need. Europe was not God's agenda for me! My benefactors, who are not Christians, in turn have been abundantly blessed.

By God's grace, I eventually purchased my own home. I had moved from loss to having more than enough! Throughout my years of waiting, never once did I fast and pray for God to do my will; rather, my prayers daily were and still are intercessory and for God to order my steps.

When we learn to place others first, we do not have to worry about self. Our Heavenly Father takes care of us. This is all about the great God we have who is ever-present with us. Prayers said by all were answered, but not according to our thinking and timing, but according to God's purpose and in HIS time.

We sometimes do make wrong turns and choices, but our gracious God is ever loving and merciful and always ready to pick us up when we fail. Praying according to His will is much easier than trying to bend God to do our will. The secret to living a life of peace and not being in want is to love God above all else, to love one another and always be ready to forgive as God forgives us.

Faith and Trust

Throughout the story, Ruth did not verbalise any form of prayer, nor did she ask for prayer or run around asking for aid. She had an inner strength that came from her deep faith in Yahweh. Faith is not a religion; religiosity kills. Faith is obedience and acting upon the revealed will and character of God. Faith is having a personal relationship with God and, in turn, a loving relationship to others. The Bible is our source for knowing God's revealed will for all of humankind.

We are all aware that something greater controls the earth and skies and everything in it. Whether or not we choose to believe God exists is a matter of personal choice. God will never force anyone to love Him. He loves us all—the good, the bad and the ugly. He created every human being to have a relationship with Him, and in His relentless love, He gave us the freedom of choice.

Every human being has been given a specific role in life, that is often missed when we think little or too much of self, which generally stems from being hurt at some time in life. Many will go about recreating themselves in the hope of finding the evasive peace and joy and even acceptance into society. The mask soon falls away, and failure and depression set in. Sometimes totally trusting God to help us overcome situations is tough. God has all the answers pertaining to life, and these will be found in the Bible.

Gideon is an example of not believing that God's plan for him was greater than what he believed himself to be. Gideon had no political ambitions and merely existed within a life of fear. When God called him to fight the Midianites and lead the Israelites out of military and moral oppression, he was reluctant to obey. He thought he was not good enough. However, despite his doubts, when he realised that God would be with him, he submitted to God's will. He was victorious and gave all the glory to God. Throughout history God has chosen the weak to demonstrate HIS power![353]

On the other hand, Joseph, the favourite son of Jacob, was an arrogant young man and boasted to his brothers, which provoked their jealousy. They sold him into slavery. Indeed, God had given him the gift of interpreting dreams but to begin with he used this gift to honour himself. Joseph had to experience life as a slave, attempted rape by Potiphar's wife and then being thrown into jail for an offence he did not commit. These were major setbacks for Joseph, but in retrospect, those hurdles were concrete steps to maturity and fame.

Despite his grim situation in prison, Joseph put aside self-interest to help others in the midst of his own suffering! Not only did he listen to their distress, he also offered to solve their problem by interpreting their dreams. Most certainly it was also a time of testing, which ultimately set him up for God's plan manifested through him.

God's favour was with Joseph, and this gave him favour in the sight of the jail keeper. The keeper gave Joseph total charge of the prisoners, a job he performed well. Sometime later, the king of Egypt's chief baker and chief cupbearer were imprisoned for committing offences against Pharaoh. Joseph was given charge of these two special prisoners. One night these two prisoners each had a dream, and Joseph was able to interpret the dreams.[354]

Two years later, Pharaoh had a dream that greatly troubled him, but none of his magicians or wise men were able to interpret the dream. The cupbearer suddenly remembered Joseph's interpretation of his dream and brought it to Pharaoh's attention. Joseph was able to interpret Pharaoh's dream and to forewarn Pharaoh of the impending famine. Pharaoh believed all that Joseph told him and made him prime minister of Egypt.[355]

Ruth found favour with God when she surrendered her life to God, and as a result, she found favour with Boaz. Ruth's surrender clearly demonstrates that finding favour with God is not limited to the spiritual realm but extends to the material realm as well. We should all desire God's favour by emulating those who have gone before us and proven nothing is impossible with God!

God longs to favour your career, your family, your marriage, those with whom you work, your colleagues, your ministry and in fact, everything that has to do with our everyday lives. Proverbs 3 tells us to trust in God and to surrender to Him. Let *hesedh* be our trademark. Only then will we find favour with both God and humanity.

The Book of Ruth
Chapter Three

ONE DAY NAOMI her mother-in-law said to her, "My daughter, should I not seek security for you,[356] that it may be well for with you?

2. Now is not Boaz our kinsman, with whose maids you were? Behold, he winnows barley at the threshing floor tonight.

3. Wash yourself therefore, and anoint yourself and put on your best clothes, and go down to the threshing floor; but do not make yourself known to the man until he has finished eating and drinking.

4. It shall be when he lies down, that you shall notice the place where he lies, and you shall go and uncover his feet and lie down; then he will tell you what you shall do."

5. She said to her, "All that you say I will do."

6. So she went down to the threshing floor and did according to all that her mother-in-law had commanded her.

7. When Boaz had eaten and drunk and his heart was merry, he went to lie down at the end of the heap of grain; and she came secretly, and uncovered his feet and lay down.

8. It happened in the middle of the night that the man was startled and bent forward; and behold, a woman was lying at his feet.

9. He said, "Who are you?" And she answered, "I am Ruth,

your maid. So spread your covering[357] over your maid, for you are a close relative."

10. And he said, "May you be blessed of the LORD, my daughter. You have shown your last kindness to be better than the first by not going after young men, whether poor or rich.

11. Now, my daughter, do not fear. I will do for you whatever you ask, for all my people in the city know that you are a woman of excellence.

12. Now it is true that I am a close relative; however, there is a closer than I.

13. Remain this night, and when morning comes, if he will redeem you, good; let him redeem you. But if he does not wish to redeem you, then I will redeem you, as the LORD lives. Lie down until the morning."

14. So she lay at his feet until the morning, but rose before one could recognise another; and he said, "Let it not be known that the woman came to the threshing floor."

15. Again he said, "Give me the cloak that is on you and hold it." So she held it, and he measured six measures of barley and laid it on her. Then she went into the city.

16. When she came to her mother-in-law, she said, "How did it go you my daughter?" And she told her all that the man had done for her.

17. She said, "These six measures of barley he gave to me, for he said, 'Do not go to your mother-in-law empty-handed.'"

18. Then she said, "Wait, my daughter, until you know how the matter turns out; for the man will not rest until he has settled it today."[358]

~

Threshing Floor

Ancient Israel was primarily an agrarian society. Agricultural practices provided a framework for the lives of many ancient Israelites. It's no accident that the Bible is filled with farming and land references and metaphors. As their main source of livelihood, agriculture was integral to the life of the Israelites. Wheat and barley were grown for bread and were staples for the Israelites.

At the end of harvest season, the harvesters and their families would pitch tents and stay near or around the threshing floor, which would have been an area of activity. Following the harvest, God commanded there be a celebration for seven days for everyone in the village to come together irrespective of position.[359]

The actual threshing floor would have been an open space possibly on high ground to take full advantage of the winds blowing through. The process of threshing was to separate the kernels from the stalks. The resulting mixture of chaff and kernels would be tossed into the air, and the wind would blow away the light chaff while the heavier kernels would fall back into the winnowing basket.

No specific details are provided in the Word of God regarding Boaz's threshing floor. We can only surmise it was an area that was open to the winds, and the floor itself was solid made of impacted earth or rocks, for the winnowed grains to be placed. Boaz would probably not have slept in the general threshing area, but in a veranda-type open area with wooden floors, where the winnowed grain was heaped for later use or storage.

The night that Ruth and Boaz spent together on the thresh-ing floor could well have resulted in the loss of reputation for both. Within the cultural context, the threshing floor is often depicted as a place of illicit behaviour, where prostitutes would offer their services to the men.

Hosea accused Israel of acting like prostitutes on the threshing floor: *"O people of Israel, do not rejoice as other nations do. For you have been unfaithful to you God, hiring yourselves out like prostitutes, worshipping other gods on every threshing floor."*[360]

The threshing floor could be likened in this day to end-of-year celebrations generally associated with organisations or even universities. During these so-called celebrations fuelled by alcohol and possibly drugs, some people use intoxication as an excuse to participate in sexual activities or even rape, the results of which are emotional damage, broken relationships, loss of employment and reputation and having to live with the guilt of indiscretion.

In biblical times threshing and winnowing were associated with blessings and judgment. The provision of grain was deep-ly rooted in their faith, and they believed the harvest was con-trolled and blessed by Yahweh. In their agrarian culture, the ancient Israelites understood themselves to be tenant farmers of the land that belongs to Yahweh: *"for the land belongs to me. You are only foreigners and tenant farmers working for me."*[361]

The threshing floor goes beyond physical sustenance and has a spiritual significance as the place where good and evil are separated. In Hosea 13:3 God's judgment on idolatrous

Ephraim was that they would be blown away like chaff. God will rescue His people and the enemies *"will be beaten and trampled like sheaves of grain on a threshing floor."*[362] The wicked will be judged and set for destruction; they will be blown away like worthless chaff scattered by the wind.[363]

For them to receive abundant blessings, Yahweh commanded the Israelites to live a life of obedience to His decrees and commandments:

> *"If you follow my decrees and are careful to obey my commands... Your threshing season will overlap with the grape harvest, and your grape harvest will overlap with the season of planting grain...I will give you peace...you will have a surplus of crops that you will need to clear out the old grain to make room for the new harvest!"*[364]

The prophet Joel spoke metaphorically of restoration and hope when a time will come where once again the threshing floor will be filled with grain. His prophecy points to the day when Jesus made a way for us to be recompensed and restored.[365]

John the Baptist pointed to Jesus as the One who would clear the threshing floor with His winnowing fork, separating the wheat from the chaff. The *wheat* depicts followers of Christ who will be gathered and filled with the Holy Spirit. The *chaff* represents the unrepentant who will burn with unquenchable fire.[366] These verses paint a metaphorical picture of the day of judgment and of heaven and hell.

In this day, threshing in developed countries has been mechanised. However, we could view the world stage as being a threshing floor where good and evil exist. We can make a choice of being "wheat" to reproduce more wheat or chaff to be blown away!

Naomi's Scheme

Naomi was aware that Elimelech did have a circle of relatives in Bethlehem, and it would not have been unusual for her to seek financial help in times of hardship, but it was not her first choice. The fact that Ruth had caught the attention of Boaz and the hesedh he had shown her was to Naomi the best way out of poverty.

Naomi would have been aware of the laws of inheritance, but the possibility of marriage between Boaz and Ruth, which in the norm was highly unlikely, did not deter her! Naomi had seven weeks to work out a plan to further her cause.

In terms of marriage to a next of kin, Naomi stood first in line, but she was genuinely concerned for Ruth. After all, in a manner, it was a let-down that her son Mahlon was unable to father a child with Ruth and worse still died without leaving any means for the young barren widow to survive.

Naomi decided to go down the risky path to marry Ruth to Boaz. Being a native of Bethlehem, Naomi would have known that at the end of harvest the men and their families would be celebrating and some of the single men would spend nights at the threshing floor, including Boaz.

Boaz was one of Naomi's close relatives, and it would have been logical for the two to marry each other or that Naomi married the other close nameless relative. Naomi, in fact, stood aside in an act of sacrificial love in her scheme to give Ruth in marriage to Boaz. Was Naomi thinking along the lines of Ruth's going to the threshing floor to seduce Boaz and trap him into marriage? Extraordinary that Naomi would even consider such a risky scheme!

Most parents, no matter what faith or religion they may profess, would not or should not attempt to marry their daughters by means of sexual immorality. We are all aware of the hurt that comes from sexual immorality, particularly adultery. Innocent children get hurt, spouses are hurt, and families—both immediate and extended—are torn apart. Anger sets in and can sometimes result in deep depression or even murder. Sexual immorality is not the route to getting a marriage proposal.

Naomi was anxious for Ruth to be married, thus fulfilling her prayer in 1:9 for her widowed daughters-in-law. Her instructions to Ruth, i.e., to have a bath and beautify herself, would be perfectly natural. The act of bathing or washing would not have been a regular occurrence in ancient Israel, and perhaps the application of perfumed oil was to soothe and soften her chapped skin and exude a pleasant fragrance.

Most women know that perfumed oil is soothing, relaxing and sensuous! Modern-day oils claim to be restorative when applied to the body, face and hair. There is nothing like a good soak in fragrant oils at the end of a long day—a luxury indeed!

In modern times, periods of mourning are still observed in various ways. For instance, in Chinese culture the immediate family wear burlap[367] on the day of the funeral and then black for up to a hundred days. Muslims would generally wear white or black and mourn for about seven to forty days. The same is observed in certain Christian denominations.

The number of days for prayers and rituals will vary according to either the wishes of the deceased or according to the wealth of the family. Traditional wealthy Chinese would burn paper mansions, cars, luxuries and loads of money for the deceased to be cared for in the afterlife. For some, the observance of wearing black or white can go on for some years until such time as they overcome the deep grief.

It is highly probable that Naomi was advising Ruth to end her period of mourning, signalling to Boaz that she was ready for marriage. A parallel may be found in 2 Samuel 12:20 when David washed himself, applied perfumed oil and changed his clothes following the death of his child borne out of his illicit relationship with Bathsheba.

A common practice in that time was to refrain from washing and anointing whilst in mourning.[368] Tamar *"took off her widow's garments"*[369] to seduce Judah, her father-in-law. He had refused to allow his youngest son Shelah to marry Tamar—from fear that Shelah too might die as did his older brothers. Out of this illicit sexual encounter, the twins Perez and Zerah were born.[370]

Tamar had married Judah's firstborn son Er, but he was wicked and died. As the Law required, Er's brother Onan had to marry Tamar to produce an heir. But Onan was not willing to have a child, and each time he was intimate with Tamar, he *"would waste his semen on the ground."*[371] God considered it evil for Onan to deny a child to his dead brother, so the Lord took Onan's life too. Tamar rightly or wrongly was determined to produce an heir to prolong the family name.

When told Tamar was pregnant, Judah indignantly demanded she be burnt to death for her immorality. However, when Judah discovered he was responsible, he was just as quick to acknowledge she was more righteous than him in his failure to give his son Shelah to her.[372] Tamar gave birth to twins and named them Perez[373] and Zerah.

The climax of Naomi's instructions was for Ruth to wait until nightfall when Boaz had fallen asleep after the harvest feast, and only then was she was to lie down and "uncover his feet."[374] As may be discerned, the narrator used provocative language that invites a multiplicity of allusions to further heighten the tension in the ensuing drama. The night-time scenario of eating and drinking hints of a situation similar to that of Lot's daughters, who seduced their father by getting him intoxicated with wine.

In fear, Lot fled Zoar with his two daughters to a cave in the mountains, following the destruction of Sodom. His two daughters decided that, to preserve the family name, they would seduce their father, as there was no one else around to impregnate them. They got Lot so drunk that he was not aware of the misdeeds of his daughters. The incestuous sexual encounter resulted in Lot's daughter's becoming the ancestors of the Moabites and Ammonites.[375]

Considering the *hesedh* previously demonstrated between Naomi and Ruth, the idea that Naomi would encourage Ruth to immoral actions like those of Lot's daughters is unacceptable.

Even if Naomi did have seduction in the back of her mind, nothing in the text points to any form of immorality on the part of Boaz or Ruth.

Indeed, Naomi had formulated a plan for Ruth to seek long-term protection from Boaz, possibly even marriage, but her scheme did not materialise as she had planned.

Ruth's Courageous Choice

Naomi's scheme for Ruth to visit the threshing floor during the night was a monumental risk. Ruth could have refused; even though it may have endangered her life, she acquiesced for Naomi's sake. Naomi's scheme at face value would have been a wrong choice even in this day.

In retrospect, these actions affirm God's ever-presence and protection. Nothing is impossible with God. No matter how much or how often we have failed, He is able to turn a bad choice or situation for good in the most unexpected ways at times alien to our thinking.

Both Ruth and Boaz were placed in a situation where moral choices had to be made. Bearing in mind Ruth's earlier oath to God and to Naomi[376] and Boaz's reverence for God,[377] to consider anything less than their high moral standards would be unthinkable.

To consider Ruth's act of uncovering and lying at Boaz's feet to mean Ruth uncovered his nakedness as a means to be intimate with Boaz, is in fact reading into the text (eisegesis) and applying one's own presupposition rather than understanding the meaning of the text. Critically, it must be noted that Boaz had to *"bend forward"* (3:8) in order to identify the person lying at his feet.

There is a marked difference between the terms *"by"* and *"with."* Lot's daughters got him drunk to *"lay with"* their father.[378] David called for Bathsheba and *"he lay with her."*[379] The consequence of this illicit union between David and Bathsheba was harsh.

Naomi's instruction to Ruth was to uncover his feet and lie down. Ruth did as she was told, but she did not lie *with* Boaz. In all probability she lay down by his feet, as Boaz had to bend forward to see who it was when he awoke.

The direct object Ruth was to *"uncover"* was Boaz's *"feet."* Had Ruth exposed Boaz's nakedness and had a sexual encounter with him, it would have placed her at the level of those prostitutes who visited the threshing floor at the end of harvest. The consequence of Ruth's submission of lying by Boaz's feet was unlimited grace and favour from God encapsulated by the term *hesedh*. Ruth's excursion to the threshing floor was not with the intention of seducing Boaz but to communicate to him her submission to serve him and to seek his protection, as may have existed according to some form of tradition.

What better way to secure the attention of a busy judge and landlord's than to make the approach at the end of a bountiful harvest when the toil was completed, and Boaz was in a relaxed state of mind!

An Eastern tradition that has long existed and still exists to denote submission and obedience is the kissing of the foot or hand. As children, once a year following the end of Ramadan and on the first day of Eid (or Hari Raya—a day of celebration as known in the Far East), we had to kneel before our parents and kiss their feet in obeisance. We children truly disliked this yearly ritual, but the day ahead of festivities and collecting money (instead of presents) from the elders soon enough made this act of submission tolerable!

It is probable that Boaz, being aware of Ruth's excellent qualities, both from what he had heard and by observing her at work in his fields could have assumed that she would not have accepted any charitable acts from him, preferring to maintain herself.[380] Positively, Naomi had to force the issue!

Sasson applies a comparison through Isaiah (Isaiah 47:2) where the object exposed is a leg (*soq* not *regel*) and states that there are enough exceptions to the rule and cautions "against rashly accusing Naomi of urging Ruth on to such acts of boldness."[381]

Traditionally, Boaz would have slept with a large mantle or cloak covering him. Naomi shrewdly figured out the uncovering of his feet in the cool night air would precipitate a chill and awaken him. Boaz was certainly startled or shivered by the uncovering of his feet.

The narrator skilfully added yet another dimension of suspense, the hour of midnight was the time given, implying the bewitching hour, a time of peril or a time of destiny.[382]

Sasson suggests that the verb *harad*[383] projects Boaz's fear of the evil spirit Lilith, who imposed herself sexually with sleeping men.[384] Legends characterise Lilith as a beautiful woman who seduces men or copulates with them in their sleep (a succubus), then spawns demon children. According to some accounts, Lilith is the Queen of Demons.[385]

Lilith originated in the ancient Near East and was identified as an evil spirit known as the "dark maid" in the Sumerian myth "The Descent of Inanna" (*c.* 2000 BC). In time, Lilith made her way into Israelite tradition. The Babylonian Talmud (Shabbat 151a) says: "It is forbidden for a man to sleep alone in a house, lest Lilith get hold of him."[386] Lilith is also featured as the queen of demons, seeking to destroy babies whilst in their mother's womb and is said to fertilise herself with male sperm to spawn more demons.

Reference to her as a vampire was inscribed on a limestone wall plaque discovered in Arslan Tash, Syria, in 1933. The tablet, dating from around the seventh or eighth century, probably hung in the home of a pregnant lady and served as an amulet against Lilith. One translation reads: "O you who fly in (the) darkened room(s), Be off with you this instant, Lilith. Thief, breaker of bones."[387] Malay folklore has a similar demon named Pontianak.

Ruth's words and actions clearly demonstrate she had no desire to break Yahweh's law to secure a marriage proposal from Boaz. Ruth's approach was devoid of any form of sexual enticement. Boaz would have appreciated Ruth's actions and request for protection.

In stark contrast to Ruth, Potiphar's wife sexually desired Joseph. Despite his repeated refusal, she pursued him daily to lie with her. So great was her lust for Joseph that in desperation she grabbed his garment and demanded he lie with her.

Joseph fled leaving his garment in her hands. Revengeful at being declined, she accused Joseph of attempted rape![388]

The Proposal

Naomi's instruction to Ruth was to wait until Boaz had finished eating and drinking and was asleep. In the stillness of the night, Ruth was to uncover Boaz's feet, lie down, and then meekly wait for Boaz to make the first move.[389] Filled with confidence, Ruth cast aside Naomi's instruction to wait in submission, and instead boldly proposed marriage. Ruth appealed to Boaz's familial status as "redeemer"[390] as a reason for him to marry her. Her need was for him to provide the much-needed economic security for herself and Naomi.

Boaz awakened from slumber, in his surprise asked the question: *"Who are you?"* Note the difference between *"Whose young woman is this?"* (1:5) and the current verse: *"Who are you?"* At this juncture, Ruth, filled with her God-given confidence, departs from Naomi's instructions and instead of waiting for Boaz to make the first move, she boldly declares herself as his handmaiden and requests that Boaz being a close relative *"spread his wings"* over her (3:10).[391] In simple terms, she is asking for his protection and marriage.

To uncover Boaz's feet, Ruth would have had to lift up the corner of his garment, and this is possibly what Naomi meant for Ruth to do to indicate her need for Boaz's protection. In no way did Naomi request Ruth to uncover Boaz's genitals. The Hebrew term *kanaph* is associated with the corner of a garment or associated with *kenapayim* ("wings of refuge"). Theologically, the terms can be associated with Boaz's earlier blessings upon Ruth when he prayed for Yahweh under whose wings she had sought refuge to *"give her a full reward"* (2:12).

Noteworthy is the way Ruth identified herself. In Ruth 2 when Boaz inquired to whom Ruth belonged, she was identified as a Moabitess from the land of Moab (2:5-7) and her self-designated status was that of a "foreigner" (*nokriya*, 2:10) and Boaz's *siphah* ("maidservant," 2:13). In the climactic scene of chapter three, Ruth omits any reference to being a Moabitess and confidently uses the term *amah* ("handmaid," 3:9), thus elevating her status and signalling her readiness not only to serve him but to be his wife.

Wings of Refuge

Seeking refuge under God's wings is found in Psalm 91. God invites us to abide and take refuge under His protection.[392] This Psalm is one I, as with many other believers, pray in times of trouble, if not daily. Not only do we have God's protection but also a firm assurance that no matter what evil swirls around us, it will not destroy us. God, in His unfailing love, will provide for all of our needs when we learn to live under His mighty wingspan.[393]

When surrounded by his enemies, King David cried out to God to hide him under the shadow of HIS wings.[394] When David fled from Saul, He cried out to God for mercy and protection: *"in the shadow of your wings I will take refuge, till the storms of destruction pass by."*[395] Under God's covering, we will experience security and rejoice in the knowledge of His unending protection and love.[396]

God has a mighty wingspan, and when we learn not to dive in for cover in time of need, but to permanently stay under His covering, we will receive divine protection. He is our *"fortress and refuge"*[397]—our protection from all evil!

Jesus lamented over Jerusalem when He walked the earth. Today the world is in the same state as Jerusalem was, if not worse. Jesus longs to protect and give comfort to us all by using the analogy of a mother hen's gathering her brood under her wings.[398] Are you willing to be gathered and to stay permanently under God's mighty wingspan?

The concept of seeking refuge under God's wing is conveyed in Ezekiel 16:8, where God speaks metaphorically regarding Israel:

> *"Later I passed by, and when I looked at you and saw that you were old enough for love, I spread the corner of my garment over you and covered your naked body. I gave you my solemn oath and entered into a covenant with you, declares the Sovereign LORD, and you became mine."*

God's relentless sanctifying love is not solely for the Israelites, but for all who choose to respond to the gentle wooing of the Holy Spirit. God wishes all of mankind to be saved. In His love for us, God gave us the freedom of choice.

The words of Roy Matheson come to mind when he speaks of Ruth serving as a "theological counterpoint" to Nehemiah who had called down curses on those who *"had married women from Ashdod, Ammon and Moab."*[399] He says the following:

Ruth reminds us that Israel's God is the God of the foreigner as well. His wing span is large enough to embrace not only people of the covenant but those like Ruth who enter from the outside... This aspect of Ruth's experience contains a powerful message.[400]

In years past, many in the church may have felt ostracised and marginalised due to social, ethnic or economic factors. Others experience sexual discrimination and harassment. In this twenty-first century, save but a few, the church has come a long way in welcoming peoples from all ethnic backgrounds—rich or poor. Women are no longer marginalised and have been welcomed into leadership roles. On March 12, 1994, 32 women were ordained as priests. In January 2015, the first female bishop, Libby Lane, was consecrated in the United Kingdom.

Sexuality

When God created male and female in the garden of Eden, He bestowed upon Adam and Eve the gift of intimacy and love. God's first command to them was to go and make babies!

God did not create male and female to reproduce like animals who copulate when in heat once or twice a year, but to give pleasure through all times and seasons. Sex is meant to be a wonderful and blessed experience between husband and wife. God's desire was for absolute unity between male and female, where two become one and are bound together, providing one another with spiritual, emotional and physical bonding resulting in pleasure, joy and peace.

Adam and Eve felt no shame in their nakedness and had

the privilege of walking with God in the garden of Eden before their act of disobedience. Their God-given union was perfect and idyllic—one of total love, sexual pleasure, and unity: "bone of my bone and flesh of my flesh."[401]

Clear instructions from God are contained in the Bible regarding the moral laws pertaining to sexual activities, which are absolute and unchangeable. Parameters were set, not because God is a spoilsport, but rather in His omniscience, He wanted to prevent humanity from getting hurt. Sex out of marriage (fornication) is destructive, as is adultery, and is a sin.[402]

Premarital sex is no guarantee of marriage. Generally speaking, the woman is always the one who tends to get hurt. Additionally, as men and women move from one sexual relationship to another, they will always carry issues from a previous relationship into the new, thus influencing what could be a beautiful relationship with hurts or perceptions from the past.

Imagine taking two pieces of coloured corrugated cardboard and gluing them together. When these two pieces are taken apart bits from each board will stick one to the other. Attempts to remove the different coloured chips will cause a tear. Repeat the procedure with a different coloured board and the original board would take on a third colour. The same goes with having different relationships, bit of past actions or memories are carried into new relationships. Oftentimes these past memories do affect relationships as comparisons are made.

Inasmuch as we have moral laws on sex, God has given us guidance on how to experience love, intimacy and fulfilment. The Song of Solomon is revelatory on God's view of love and sexuality for married couples. The bride is deeply in love and longs for the caresses of her husband. In turn, the husband is totally in love and captivated by her beauty. Their language towards each other is sensual and very much focussed on one another.

Prior to being born again and studying the Scriptures, I was sexually immoral. I knew adultery was a sin and believed that, as a single person, it was acceptable to be in a sexual relationship as long as I did not commit adultery. I soon enough learnt fornication was just as bad!

Only when I truly accepted Jesus as Lord of my life did I realise what it means to be forgiven of my past sins and to have been transplanted from the kingdom of darkness into the kingdom of light.[403] It is noticeable that many churches seem almost afraid to preach on sin and repentance. Would it be for fear of losing congregants?

If you have messed up like I did, be assured that when you acknowledge your sin and repent, God will readily forgive you and bless you with abundance.[404] God loves us more than any human being can and wants the best for us.[405] Once forgiven, God blots out all our sins forever, and we are set free of all the things that have kept us in bondage.[406] Jesus said, *"If you hold to my teaching, you are truly my disciples, then you will know the truth and the truth will set you free."*[407]

Ruth sets a perfect example on how and what it means to be appealing to a potential husband. She had a strong conviction regarding her faith, in that no attempts were made to seduce Boaz. Ruth was not self-giving; her focus was, first and foremost, to provide for Naomi despite having to work at the lowest level of sweat and toil, a menial task indeed.

Ruth did not in any way appear to be seductive in order to secure a marriage; on the contrary, it did seem at the time of going to the threshing floor that she needed a bath and change out of her mourning clothes![408] Ruth's beauty and attraction radiated from within—not by external means. She was a woman of strength and humility.

If you are in the position of wanting to get married, hard as it may sound, be true to yourself. Get off social media and spend the time making lives around you better by serving in the community. Be natural, enjoy and use your God-given body, mind, spirit and talents to the fullest. Have you ever wondered why those you may consider rather plain in looks receive marriage proposals?

Our faith is not about what we outwardly profess; rather, it is about what is within us that motivates and is attractive. I am not referring to works, but of a faith that causes us to spontaneously think of others before self. If we care for others, God will surely take care of our every need. As I have already mentioned, open hands will receive abundant blessings; a clenched fist has no space to receive.

Jesus gives us the answer! He called us to be *"salt of the earth...and the light of the world."* When we cease to be what we are not and choose instead to work towards using our God-given gifts radiating from within, we will become attractive to all! Internal beauty comes from having compassion, humility and love for others determined not by speech but by our spontaneous loving deeds.[409]

Jesus urges: *"Let your light shine before men that they may see your good deeds and praise your Father in Heaven."*[410] We are made in the image of God to represent Him—to be His hands and feet, showing love and compassion in this harsh, broken world.

Kinsman Redeemer

It is debatable as to whether Ruth was aware of the complexities involved regarding her request, but she was probably aware in a general sense of Levirate laws, which she presumably would have learned from Naomi. Factually, the Levirate law did not apply to Ruth.

The central theme of *hesedh* comes to fore in Boaz's positive response to Ruth. Instead of rejection, Boaz invokes divine blessings upon Ruth: *"Blessed are you of the LORD,"*[411] in a form identical to that which Naomi expressed upon him: *"Blessed be he of the Lord...."*[412] Furthermore, in this, his blessing of Ruth, the audience would have easily recalled that which he uttered on their first meeting:

> *"I've been told all about what you have done for your mother-in-law since the death of your husband—how you left your father and mother and your homeland and came to live with a people you did not know before. May the LORD repay you for what you have done. May you be richly rewarded by the LORD the God of Israel, under whose wings you have come to take refuge."*[413]

The phrase *"blessed are you of the LORD"* is really an acknowledgement that God has not ceased in showing His abundant grace and mercy. As Block rightly comments, one who had been seduced in the middle of the night would hardly have expressed it![414] Here is to be noted the human tripartite movement of praise, blessings and actions *(hesedh)*, which was the conduit for God to move powerfully in their empty lives and turn it into an abundance of blessings beyond human expectations.

God was the key player throughout, silently but surely controlling the whole course of events. Ruth's better *hesedh* opened the floodgates that resulted in her fame as a founding mother of the Davidic dynasty.[415] God does not discriminate. In God's mercy, graciousness and love *(hesedh)*, He blessed the union of Ruth, a foreigner, and Boaz to represent the whole of His people. Indeed, the idea of good deeds and reward plays a prominent role but keeping in mind that faith and good works are interrelated, and every gift from God is by grace is important.[416]

Neither Boaz nor Ruth were under any obligation to marry each other as the constraints of the Levirate law were not applicable. Boaz's statement that Ruth's act of *hesedh*[417] is better than the first,[418] may be understood in terms of the first being Ruth's love, loyalty, care and support of Naomi.

Boaz explicates that Ruth's latter and better *hesedh* was that she had chosen him rather than from the variety of eligible virile young men *(habbehurim)* both rich and poor in the village. Without a doubt, Boaz was flattered, and he responded by assuring Ruth he would deal with her request the very same day.

According to rabbinic literature, Boaz was eighty years old and died shortly after fathering Obed,[419] thus Ruth's willingness to marry a man possibly old enough to be her father goes way beyond her personal needs. The marriage primarily was to ensure security for Naomi in every sense of the word. Ruth remained true to the oath that she swore in 1:16-17, both to Naomi and to Yahweh, and in doing so, she considered her needs least of all.

Equality of Men and Women

Boaz was certainly flattered and possibly had already loved Ruth for what she was. Being a man of honour, Boaz was conscious of another man who was a closer relative not so much to Ruth, but to Naomi, and as such, he had first refusal. Boaz assured Ruth he would do all that she had requested with the words, *"do not fear"*[420] as one way or another Ruth's desire for a husband would be fulfilled.

Furthermore, Boaz quelled her fears of possible recriminations that could have arisen with regard to her Moabite origins and perhaps having spent the night at the threshing floor by assuring her all the people of his town (3:11) regarded her as a worthy woman *(eset hayil)*. Indeed, Ruth's reputation of excellence went before her.

It is significant that Boaz uses the term *eset hayil* (woman of strength) to describe Ruth's reputation, which was common knowledge to all the people of Bethlehem. The term, *eset hayil,* is best understood in Proverbs 31, which describes the ideal wife as a woman who is virtuous, economically successful and faces life with optimistic confidence. She is a woman who multi-tasks by not only providing care for the family whilst at the same time as having a successful career.

The ideal wife as described in Proverbs 31 must be understood in terms of a wife whose exemplary conduct is not one of subservience, but rather that of a wife who is much to be admired and who enhances rather than diminishes her husband's reputation. These character traits may further be extended to all women and are not exclusive to wives! Of significance is verse 31: *"Let her own works praise her in the gates."* It was at the *"gates"* that the people gave Ruth recognition and acceptance.

Whilst Proverbs 31 may refer to a wife, it is well to note that her husband is also a man of honour, supportive and of excellent repute (v. 23). Her husband and children are full of admiration for her as a wife and mother (v. 28). Here we see a beautiful family knitted together in the love of God and for one another.

Ruth was single, she stood alone with no support group, and, in the initial stages of her arrival in Bethlehem, she was ignored. The choices she made were risky whilst at the same time she never lost sight of her oath to Naomi, which was not simply allegiance to Naomi, but was also her confession of faith.[421]

> *"For where you go I will go, and where you lodge I will lodge. Your people shall be my people, and your God my God. Where you die I will die, and there will I be buried. May the Lord do so to me and more also if anything but death parts me from you"* (Ruth 1:16-18).

Likewise in 2:1 the narrator describes Boaz as *gibbor hayil* meaning "a mighty man of valour, a hero with ability, considerate, successful, noble, wealthy," and with many other character traits that may be noted of him in the narrative. It would not be out of place to say that Ruth was the female counterpart to Boaz with the same character traits.

Although Ruth was neither rich nor prominent, the expression breaks down the dividing walls of race, culture, economic and social status between them that had hitherto existed. Indeed, for all Ruth had accomplished to this point, makes her worthy of being recognised as a woman of great courage, nobility, strength and wholesome values and places her at par with Boaz.

Women in Leadership

Whilst there is a massive push by egalitarians for advancing the equality between men and women in this day, it's not as such a new movement. Scripture has always supported the equality of men and women rather than a hierarchy. Had the Bible been heeded, it can clearly be seen that God not only honoured women, but He placed them in positions of leadership both in the Old and New Testament.

Several women who occupy leadership positions, such as Deborah, a wife and prophet whom God raised to lead Israel in a time of turbulence and violence. As judge and prophet, she exercised judicial, religious, political and spiritual authority over Israel. She accompanied Barak, her rather insecure military commander, into a successful military campaign against Sisera. Under her leadership, Israel experienced forty years of peace.[422]

Jael, the wife of Heber the Kenite, on seeing the fleeing Sisera graciously invited him into her tent. She gave him a jug of milk and made him comfortable. When Sisera fell asleep, Jael bravely drove a tent peg into his skull that went right through into the ground killing him, thus adding the final touch to Deborah's victorious military campaign.[423]

In the eighteenth year of his reign, King Josiah learned that the Book of the Law (the Torah) had been discovered in the temple. Upon hearing the words of the Law, Josiah tore his clothes in repentance as Judah had neglected and strayed from God's Law. He called for a prophet to confirm the authenticity and interpret the words of the scroll.

During this time the prophets Jeremiah, Nahum, Habakkuk and Zephaniah were serving Him. However, God directed Hilkiah the high priest and Shaphan the scribe to select Huldah the prophetess from Jerusalem. Clearly, she had the complete respect and confidence of these men. Huldah, who was used by God to voice His judgment and prophecy on Judah,[424] sparked a national revival!

Women played an equally important role in in the New Testament. They were just as much disciples in leadership as were the men, and even more so as they helped bankroll Jesus' ministry. Mary Magdalene (of Magdala)[425] was a wealthy single woman, who was under demonic strongholds until Jesus delivered her of seven demons. Thereon, in utter gratitude, she dedicated her life to Jesus both financially and spiritually. She stood by Jesus in His darkest hours, whilst others had fled, and she was the first to encounter Jesus and proclaim His resurrection.

Joanna, the wife of Chuza, was the manager of Herod's household and was in an extremely influential position and wealthy. Susanna, who was not married, was also wealthy in her own right. Many unnamed women travelled with Jesus and His disciples and *"were helping them out of their own means."*[426]

Peter went to the house of Mary, the mother of John Mark, who led a house church, when he was miraculously freed from prison.[427] Chloe of Corinth[428] and Nympha of Laodicea[429] were also leaders of their house churches. These women of character defied imposed convention and fearlessly stepped through open doors that God provided.

Scripture sets forth examples for us to follow. Clearly the path to success is to lead a life that radiates *hesedh*. It is not about being religious, but we need to have the character traits outlined in Galatians 5:22. Selflessness is the key to finding favour both with God and those around us.

The Gift of Barley

Various speculations have been proffered as to the reason for the gift of barley from Boaz. Some see it as a ruse to divert gossip in the event Ruth was discovered leaving the fields in the early hours of the morning. Perhaps it was a measure of good faith or an act of betrothal. Most likely, as it was the end of the harvest, the gift of grain was to ensure that Ruth and Naomi would have enough food, whilst he held counsel regarding their future.

Boaz did not state the reason for the gift. Yet again, we see the compassionate and caring nature of Ruth for her mother-in-law. Ruth, in her wisdom, stretched the truth slightly, by including Naomi as a co-recipient of the gift of barley. The gift can certainly be equated to Boaz's earlier concern not only for

Ruth, but like Ruth, also for Naomi. Ruth verbalised the purpose of the gift of barley: *"These six measures of barley he gave to me, for he said to me, 'You must not go back empty-handed to your mother-in-law' "* (3:17).[430] The giving of grain was but a foretaste of the fullness that was to be divinely bestowed upon all three of the protagonists. Campbell draws attention to the fact that every leading and guiding term within the story "relates a key theological theme to the action of God and to the action of the human figures who dominate the story."[431]

The Book of Ruth
Chapter Four

THEN BOAZ WENT up to the gate and sat down there, and behold, the close relative of whom Boaz spoke was passing by, so he said, "Turn aside, friend, sit down here." And he turned aside and sat down.

2. He took ten men of the elders of the city and said, "Sit down here." So they sat down.

3. Then he said to the closest relative, "Naomi, who has come back from the land of Moab, has to sell the piece of land which belonged to our brother Elimelech.

4. So I thought to inform you, saying, 'Buy it before those who are sitting here, and before the elders of my people. If you will redeem it, redeem it; but if not, tell me that I may know; for there is no one but you to redeem it, and I am after you.'" And he said, "I will redeem it."

5. Then Boaz said, "On the day you buy the field from the hand of Naomi, you also acquire Ruth the Moabitess, the widow of the deceased, in order to raise up the name of the deceased on his inheritance."

6. Then the closest relative said, "I cannot redeem it for myself, because I would jeopardize my own inheritance. Redeem it for yourself; you may have my right of redemption, for I cannot redeem it."

7. Now this was the custom in former times in Israel concerning the redemption and the exchange of land to confirm any matter: a man removed his sandal and gave it to another; and this was the manner of attestation in Israel.

8. So the closest relative said to Boaz, "Buy it for yourself." And he removed his sandal.

9. Then Boaz said to the elders and all the people, "You are witnesses today that I have bought from the hand of Naomi all that belonged to Elimelech and all that belonged to Chilion and to Mahlon.

10. Moreover, I have acquired Ruth the Moabitess, the widow of Mahlon, to be my wife, to raise up the name of the deceased on his inheritance, so that the name of the deceased will not be cut off from his brothers and from the court of his birth place; you are witnesses today."

11. Then all the people who were in the court, and the elders, said, "We are witnesses. May the LORD make the woman, who is coming into your home, like Rachel and Leah, both of whom built up the house of Israel; and may you achieve wealth in Ephrathah and become famous in Bethlehem.

12. Moreover, may your house be like the house of Perez, whom Tamar bore to Judah, through the offspring which the LORD will give you by this young woman."

13. So Boaz took Ruth, and she became his wife, and he went in to her. And the LORD enabled her to conceive, and she gave birth to a son.

14. Then the women said to Naomi, "Blessed is the LORD, who has not left you without a redeemer today, and may his

name become famous in Israel.

15. May he also be to you a restorer of life and a sustainer of your old age; for your daughter-in-law, who loves you and is better to you than seven sons, has given birth to him."

16. Then Naomi took the child and laid him in her lap, and became his nurse.

17. The neighbor women gave him a name, saying, "A son has been born to Naomi!" So they named him Obed. He was the father of Jesse, the father of David.

18. Now these are the generations of Perez: to Perez was born Hezron,

19. and to Hezron was born Ram, and to Ram Amminadab,

20. and to Amminadab was born Nahshon, and to Nahshon, Salmon,

21. and to Salmon was born Boaz, and to Boaz, Obed,

22. and to Obed was born Jesse, and to Jesse, David.[432]

The City Gates

In biblical times, apart from protecting the city against invaders, city gates were a place where important activities—both practical and divine—took place. City gates had built-in chambers. At the city gates business transactions were conducted as well as a place where a legal court would be convened to settle disputes and or have judgment passed.[433]

At the gate of Sodom, Lot met the two angels.[434] By the city gate, King David mustered his troops for battle.[435] David waited between two gates when he received the news that his son Absalom was dead.[436] Whilst in mourning for Absalom, Joab persuaded King David to take his place at the gate to signal the end of his mourning and to serve his people again.[437] Wisdom takes her stand by the gates as she cries out to all giving instructions on how to live a fulfilled life.[438] The foundation of wisdom is God Himself.

In the third of Jesus' *"I Am"* statements,[439] He shifts from being the Shepherd to using the metaphor of being a gatekeeper and the door.[440] Jesus' hearers would know that at the end of the day when the sheep return to the fold after a day of being in the fields, the shepherd would count and tend to those who have been hurt. Safely in the pen, the shepherd would lie across the entrance to protect the sheep from intruders.

The meeting at the gate refers to the gathering of a legal panel that was responsible for the people of the town. Boaz called ten men so as to constitute a legal forum, and their presence was to notarise and validate the proceedings he wished to set in motion.[441] Rabbinic literature defines the elders at the gate as the Sanhedrin.

The Exchange

Whilst the intention of this book is not to provide an excursus into the technical and legal problems linked to Levirate marriage, a brief summary is necessary to demonstrate Boaz's role as redeemer *(goël)*, first expressed by Ruth and Naomi[442] and then by Ruth[443] when she proposed marriage.

Although Naomi was portrayed as being destitute when she arrived in Bethlehem, she still retained the rights to a parcel of land that belonged to Elimelech. Perhaps at the time, she was so consumed by her tragic circumstance she had forgotten this provision, though one may presume in her plan for Ruth, she did become aware of her inheritance from Elimelech. By moving from self-centredness to showing motherly love and concern for Ruth, Naomi moved from desolateness into abundant blessings.

Bearing in mind Boaz's presumed status of judge, he was careful to act within the accepted custom and law. The rites performed by Boaz, when compared to biblical data pertaining to Levirate laws in Genesis 38, Leviticus 25:25-34 and Deuteronomy 25:5-10, have virtually no similarities; however, the assumption of the marriage duty of a *go'el* in Ruth does seem to suggest that such a custom may have existed for the story to have credibility.[444]

The nameless kinsman *(Peloni Almoni)*[445] just so happened to walk by at the gates where Boaz and the elders were holding court, and they invited the nameless relative to sit with them. The *Peloni Almoni* was given first refusal to purchase the parcel of land owned by Elimelech. He indicated his willingness to do so for his own personal gain.

However, when Boaz brought to fore that he would also have to acquire (marry) Ruth as part of the deal, the nearer kinsman declined. Boaz had reasoned that the marriage was to *"perpetuate the name of the dead through his inheritance,"*[446] he was in fact appealing to the nearer kinsman to take up the voluntary responsibility of family restoration and succour.

If the *Peloni Almoni* had agreed to redeem the clan, certainly

Boaz's promise to Ruth and Naomi would still have been met. However, the *Peloni Almoni* declines and cedes his role of redeemer to Boaz. His very words: "*I cannot redeem it myself, lest it ruin my own inheritance...*"[447]

The nearer kinsman was fearful of losing what he had. If he had agreed to marry Ruth, who was young and fertile, there was every possibility she would birth a son. The offspring would be heir to the nearer kinsman's property and would carry the name of Mahlon. Thus, in preserving Mahlon's name, the Peloni Almoni would lose the preservation of his own family name.

Rabbinic literature claims that even though female Moabites were officially permitted to marry Israelites, the *Peloni Almoni* did not know his Torah and feared that he too, like Mahlon, might die for the sin of marrying a Moabitess or that the sin might be visited on his children.[448]

The nearer redeemer would probably not have minded marrying Naomi as she was old and no longer of a childbearing age and would prove to be of no threat to his personal wealth or perpetuating his family name. In fact, he would acquire Naomi's property. The surprise element introduced by Boaz to outsmart the nearer redeemer was the substitution of Ruth for Naomi!

When the *Peloni Almoni* relinquished his rights as a kinsman-redeemer, the symbolic removal of the sandal would have been according to a custom that the elders and people would have understood.[449] The ritual of removing the sandal does appear in Deuteronomy 25:9 in relation to the preservation of the family name. However, the circumstances in Ruth differ significantly.

The Deuteronomy text stipulates that the widow is the one who goes to the gates to speak to the elders. The rejected widow removes the sandal from the wearer and spits in his face to signal freedom from obligation. It would not be far from the truth to say it was an act of humiliation and disgrace both for the person rejecting and his clan. In this instance, neither Ruth nor Naomi was present, and, strictly speaking, the law devolved upon a brother-in-law.[450]

Boaz exercised his rights, which were ceded to him by the *Peloni Almoni*. by declaring that he had redeemed all that belonged to Elimelech, Chilion and Mahlon from Naomi's hand, and his purpose in marrying (acquiring) Ruth was *"to perpetuate the name of the dead."*[451]

Boaz's act of redemption marked the end of Ruth's widowhood and infertility,[452] and notably, her social progression from the status of "foreigner" *(nokriya)*[453] to "wife" [(issa)] as she was fully accepted into the covenant community of Israel.[454] His earlier benediction that the Lord blesses her and grants her full reward was fulfilled.

Naomi's earlier prayer that the Lord deal kindly with Ruth and that Ruth would find a husband was granted,[455] but it did require the action of Naomi surrendering her usufruct rights. As Campbell rightly observes: "The wish connected to Yahweh's activity becomes fulfilled by the human protagonist."[456]

We are made in the image of God, and we are commanded to love one another. It's the kind of *agapé* love, which is in

CRITICAL CHOICE IN TIMES OF CRISIS

alignment with the sacrificial love when God sent us Christ[457] and, in turn, because of His great love for us, Christ made the ultimate sacrifice. It was not something that was pleasant! So too for us—sacrificial love is not a feeling but a firm decision of our will to help another in need no matter how difficult it may be.

I passionately believe through my own personal experience that God takes care of our every need. Every prayer is answered, but at times not according to what we want. God protects and supernaturally comforts us in times of trials and even prepares us for such times. However, for God to make a move, we need to partner with Him by our actions. Sacrificial love brings untold blessings both to the giver and recipient.

Attempting to force God to meet our demands with the "I-want, give-me, and-I-need" attitude when in prayer is futile. When our arms are opened wide and we are praying beyond our self-centredness and taking care of others, God, without our even asking, will bless us beyond measure in more ways than one.

We don't have to wait to go to heaven to have a life of abundance; it has already been given here on earth. Jesus said He came to give us life in abundance,[458] and nowhere does Jesus say we have to wait until we go to heaven!

You could make a choice to change—serve God by serving others with love and humility and learning to trust God. Confidently, I can say to you our Heavenly Father will give you peace without measure no matter what the circumstance!

We are commanded to *"do nothing out of selfish ambition or vain conceit. Rather, in humility value others above your-*

selves, not looking to your own interests but each of you to the interests of the others."[459]

The Prophetic

The all-male gathering at the gate witnessed Boaz's commitment to buy the land from Naomi, marry Ruth and perpetuate the name of the dead. The public meeting concluded with the prophetic witness statement by the men calling on Yahweh to give the same fecundity to Ruth as He did to Rachel and Leah.

Striking is the association of Ruth to Rachel and Leah, particularly in the light of the explicit reference to her ethnicity because Isaac had charged Jacob not to marry a non-Israelite.[460] The theological implications of Ruth's acceptance into the covenant community are far-reaching.

Both Rachel and Leah could not conceive initially, but the Lord opened their wombs.[461] Leah, the mother of Judah[462] is an ancestor to the tribe of Boaz and Naomi. Together with their servants Bilhah and Zilpah, they bore Jacob twelve sons from whom sprang the twelve tribes of Israel.[463]

God chose Perez to carry the family line of Judah, which ultimately culminates in the birth of the Messiah. The people at the gate would have understood the blessing of Perez when they blessed Boaz to be like Perez. At the time, none of them would have known that Perez and Boaz were part of the lineage that leads to Christ Jesus who was born some 1,700 years later.

The benediction naturally progresses in the wish for prosperity and fame directed at Boaz. The building up of the house of Israel was fulfilled by Boaz's offspring, who became the grandfather of King David, foreshadowing the rise of the Davidic dynasty[464] and ultimately in the promised seed of Genesis 3:15:

> *"And I will put enmity*
> *Between you and the woman,*
> *And between your seed and her Seed;*
> *He shall bruise your head,*
> *And you shall bruise His heel."*[465]

Some twenty-eight generations later, this promise culminated in the virgin birth of Christ Jesus![466]

Barrenness to Blessings

The marriage of Boaz and Ruth resulted in the birth of a son and heir, Obed. Ruth's singular mind of doing *hesedh* to Naomi moved her from loss of husband and ten years of infertility to being the wife of Boaz and the mother of Obed.

Upon facing a crisis, Ruth could have chosen to revert to her old lifestyle of financial wealth. However, rather than instant gratification, she chose to move into uncharted territory. In her quiet and unassuming faith, Ruth humbled herself and sought refuge under God's mighty wingspan.[467]

The choices Ruth made were also life-changing for Naomi. Seen in the light of Naomi's lament of being brought back empty, God had indeed done hesedh to her by blessing her way beyond her expectations. The loss of her two sons was singularly replaced by Ruth whose, as the women proclaimed, worth was *"better than seven sons."*[468]

The number seven represents perfection. The birth of

Obed[469] gave Naomi the longed-for "redeemer" who would not only preserve the family name but would also provide for her for the rest of her life.

The miraculous turn from loss, grief, famine and despair to a life of abundance beyond expectations was made possible not just by words but by the demonstration of extraordinary *hesedh* initially by Ruth, then Boaz and Naomi.

Ruth's *hesedh* towards Naomi changed her mother-in-law from a bitter, selfish woman to one who learnt what it truly means to be loved and to love. Dynamics change radically when we turn from self-centredness and look to caring for others. *Agapé* love changes lives.

Indeed, it was not just limited to the redemption of a small family in Bethlehem, but rather the continuance of redemptive history that extends far beyond the narrator's time and place. As a result, God was able to exercise His rule in the lives of these ordinary people, by honouring them as the ancestors of Israel's greatest King, and even more so, that of the King of kings and Lord of Lords, Jesus Christ!

Fulfillment

The conclusion of the narrative provides a genealogy that reaches back to Tamar and Judah and the birth of Perez. Indeed, the narrator looks even further back when Ruth is acknowledged alongside the patriarchal family to women like Rachel and Leah.[470] Moving ahead, the narrative establishes the lineage of David and as is apparent in the New Testament, culminating in the birth of the promised Messiah.[471]

Ruth is elevated alongside Tamar, Rahab and the *"wife of Uriah"* in a list of forty-two generations of male ancestors of *"Joseph the husband of Mary, of whom Jesus was born, who is called the Messiah."*[472] Whilst there is no doubt as to the divine selection of the above-named women, there is a fair amount of diversity regarding their selection.

Tamar not unlike Ruth was widowed and childless but preserved the lineage by her devious sexual encounter with Judah. Although discerning *hesedh* in her actions is difficult, she was acknowledged as being more righteous than Judah in the need to preserve the family line of Judah's son.[473] Rahab, the mother of Boaz, although a former prostitute, was considered a heroine because she showed *hesedh* in protecting the Israelites.[474] A proselyte like Ruth, she is upheld as a model of faith.[475]

Not all rabbinic literature condemns Bathsheba who was guilty of adultery and indirectly responsible for the murder of her husband Uriah. Her actions were quite the opposite of hesedh![476] However, she ultimately gave birth to Solomon, who through her intervention succeeded David.[477] It is unsustainable that Ruth, apart from being a proselyte, was guilty of sexual immorality.

It is apparent God can and will use those whom society condemns or judges as sinners to fulfil His purpose. We need only to read the "Hall of Faith" in the eleventh chapter of Hebrews to see that God used the weakest and worst to fulfil His purpose. One element they all had in common was faith.

A beautiful, tender scene is depicted when *"Naomi took the child and laid him on her bosom, and became a nurse to him."*[478]

The act of placing Obed to her lap and nursing him does not mean Naomi physically breastfed Obed. "Nurse" is a translation from the Hebrew *aman*, which means "to uphold, support and nourish." Amongst the various translations of *aman*, none of them depict physical breastfeeding.[479]

The placing of Obed on her lap dates back for centuries, right up to modern times! Traditionally, in Middle and Far Eastern countries, babies are placed on laps and gently rocked to sleep. The mother or person would sit cross-legged on the floor, and the child would be placed with its head resting on the knee area and that part of the leg would move gently up and down. Older siblings would also care for the baby in this manner. It is an extremely safe and relaxed method for carer and child, rather than standing up and bouncing the baby or child up and down.

Inasmuch as the women proclaimed Obed would sustain and nourish Naomi in her old age, as *aman* (could also mean foster mother) to her grandson, Naomi would also sustain and nourish her grandson physically with food and spiritually by guiding and teaching him in the ways of Yahweh.

It is not uncommon for believing parents and grandparents to ensure from the time of birth or even prior to pray for a baby. At baptism godparents are chosen to support the child's spiritual growth and wellbeing. As the child grows, without a doubt, faith and trust in Christ would be instilled. These days it is fashionable to have godparents who are not believers, are wealthy, and sadly, lacking in faith.

To describe the beautiful loving scene of Naomi's holding

Obed close to her heartbeat is well-nigh impossible. It is not unusual for maternal (or paternal) grandmothers to take over the physical care of a newborn baby, particularly in the first forty days of confinement. In this modern day in the name of "independence," those who can afford it seek out the services of a qualified nurse or doula.

Traditionally, in Eastern families, following the birth of a child, the mother is confined to the home for forty days. During this period, a strict diet is imposed, one aspect of which is steaming a whole small chicken with fresh ginger and herbs drunk daily. The process of steaming the chicken will yield a tiny cup of soup packed with nutrients.

More importantly, during this period of confinement, the family, rich or poor, will take all necessary steps to ensure the new mother is pampered. It is also a time of bonding for the new family unit. Postnatal depression was unheard of in my time. There was no such thing as lack of sleep. The mother of the baby would do the night feeds and sleep during the day whilst family took over the care of the infant. Husbands would be out at work, returning to a peaceful loving household. With independence, unless one can afford nurses or nannies, having a baby can be stressful without support from family or friends.

Naomi, in holding Obed to her bosom as *aman*, should be an encouragement to us all of the importance of doing *hesedh* to one another. The foreigner Ruth was accepted and valued. In the same manner, I urge all in-laws to desist from all forms of criticism and jealousy and start practising *hesedh*.

We were all created to live as a loving community. No one

person living on this earth should ever feel isolated. Our responsibility is to take care of those around us. Time is a precious commodity, and we need to share our time with others.

> "There is one who scatters, and yet increases all the more,
>   And there is one who withholds what is justly due,
>   and yet it results only in want.
>   The generous man will be prosperous,
>   And he who waters will himself be watered."[480]

Epilogue
The Grace of God

H AS GOD LOST His power and control? Certainly not! In His great love for us, He gave us the freedom of choice. *El* (as in *El Shaddai*) is often used to denote God's power to interpose into any situation.[481] These characteristics of God are clearly demonstrated in the Bible throughout the ages and are also a present, continuing experience. The Hebrew term *hesedh* encapsulates the power, love, mercy and compassion of *El Shaddai* in the divine/human relationship.

In the New Testament, Paul uses the Greek term *charis* (grace) no less than 101 times. Oftentimes Paul opens and closes his letters with a prayer that God will bestow grace upon his readers. *Charis* has various implications relating to God's power, love, compassion, will and purpose for humankind, namely salvation wrought by the ultimate sacrificial love of Christ on the cross.

As Schreiner writes:

Grace in Pauline theology is not merely a gift but also a power that transforms. Paul testifies, *"by the grace of God I am what I am"* (1 Cor. 15:10). The change in Paul's life can be ascribed only to the grace of God…Grace has ordained that believers will do good works (Eph. 2:10)…

For Paul, living under grace does not translate into freedom to pursue one's autonomous will.[462]

I truly believe that God answers every prayer of need. But at times these prayers seem to be either delayed or unanswered. It is not because God has ignored us; rather, it is because He knows a better way, which somehow may not fit into our carnal thinking.

We, who are able, need to act on God's behalf in the realm of earthly matters. Jesus explains what is expected of a believer in Mathew 25:35-45, when He invites those who acted on His behalf to take up their inheritance. He said:

> "For I was hungry and you gave me something to eat, I was thirsty and you gave me something to drink...I needed clothes and you clothed me... I tell you the truth, whatever you did for one of the least of these brothers of mine, you did for me...whatever you did not do for one of the least of these you did not do for me."

It is imperative as believers to understand that our mandate is to take care of those that Christ has placed before us; we are to be His mouthpiece. The need to be supported, loved and accepted is a worldwide and sometimes fatal malady and is no respecter of gender, wealth, race or religion. Every human being is a unique creation created by God who is the epitome of love, grace and mercy. Our very souls, when devoid of this inheritance, will be filled with greed, envy and a sense of emptiness, which are weapons of self-destruction.

These weapons of destruction and strongholds can be demolished because the battle is not against flesh and blood, but against wrong thought patterns and ideas. Humankind by nature is weak and subjected, oftentimes to sin as an easy route to a temporary feel-good factor, which is not only self-destructive but ripples onwards touching the lives of others.

Dunn expresses:

> The key to a right understanding of the human condition is of humankind as a creation of the one creator God… The need to satisfy natural desires is a point of strength if it reinforces creaturely dependence on God. But humankind as a whole has turned its back on God, seeking to live out of its own wisdom. And what should have been a point of strength has become a means of enslavement.[483]

Dunn aptly makes the point that sin is the force that causes rebellion against God. In the attempt to satisfy the desires of the flesh, religion as in one's personal belief is used as a substitute for God. The fullness of life as intended by God is one that is regulated by God. "Under the twin powers of sin and death, even God's good law has been manipulated and corrupted, and the result is human enslavement and social factionalism and embitterment."[484]

God has not left us defenceless. Prayer is the most powerful weapon that any believer could possess. Prayer is having a normal conversation with God; it is a means of communicating and developing a close relationship with God. Prayer unleashes the power, wisdom, love and mercy of God. To ignore the global crisis is tantamount to disobedience.[485] We need to intercede passionately, because prayer brings life and reaches where even the most advanced weapons for warfare cannot.

Paul, as a Pharisee, was zealous for his religion and was intent on persecuting Christians.[486] He approved the murder of Stephen and watched as Stephen was stoned to death.[487] He would go into home churches and drag the men and women to prison.[488]

His very breath spewed murder against the followers of Christ, and, with murder on his mind, he journeyed on to Damascus in search of Christians.[489] On the road to Damascus, he had a dramatic encounter with Christ, which was life-changing.[490] No doubt the followers of Christ would have been praying for protection and even possibly for Paul to encounter Christ!

This change in Paul's life can only be ascribed to the grace of God. The logic of Paul's conversion was that he was subjected to the law, which was inadequate. He had a religion that subscribed to murder, which he presumed was acceptable before a holy and compassionate God. Paul had a dramatic encounter with Christ, and, in a flash, he experienced the unmerited grace of God.[491]

Manasseh was truly evil. Not only was he idolatrous, he practised witchcraft, sorcery and divination. He went a step further and sacrificed his own sons to worthless idols.[492] God sent the Assyrian army to take him away. Manasseh was bound in chains and literally had a hook put through his nose and was dragged away to Babylon. In his profound distress, Manasseh humbled himself, and God moved and restored his kingship.[493] The providence of God as seen in redemptive history has not ceased.

We are all part of this grand golden scheme of God's redemption for humankind, irrespective of race, colour, gender, profession, offenders, the poor and the rich. In a world shaken by war, famine, pestilence and fear, now more than ever, we need to repent and receive the gift of God's grace.[494]

> *"When I shut up heaven and there is no rain,*
> *or command the locusts to devour the land,*
> *or send pestilence among my people,*
> *if My people who are called by My name*
> *will humble themselves, and pray and seek my face,*
> *and turn from their wicked ways,*
> *then I will hear from heaven, will forgive their sin*
> *and heal their land."*[495]

Endnotes

Introduction

[1] Deuteronomy 31:6; Hebrews 13:5.

[2] Hosea 4:6.

[3] Ronald M. Hals, *The Theology of the Book of Ruth* (Philadelphia: Fortress Press, 1969), 16.

[4] Roy Matheson, "The Hebrew Short Story: A Study of Ruth," in *Teach Me Your Paths: Studies in Old Testament Literature and Theology*, Edited by John Kessler and Jeffrey Greenman (Toronto: Clements Publishing, 2001), 227.

[5] Romans 8:28 (NASB).

[6] Timothy 3:16.

[7] Matthew 5:44.

[8] Proverbs 12:25.

[9] Philippians 4:6.

[10] Philippians 2:14; Proverbs 15:1.

[11] Galatians 5:13.

[12] Malachi 3:16; Numbers 23:19.

[13] Ruth 1:6.

[14] Ruth 4:13.

[15] Deuteronomy 6:4-9.

[16] NKJV. Those of the Jewish faith are required to recite the Shema twice a day. We would do well to do likewise.

[17] Matthew 22:34-39; Luke 10:27-28 (NASB).

[18] John 13:34 (NKJV).

[19] See Otto J. Baab, *The Theology of The Old Testament* (Nashville, Tennessee: Abingdon Press, 1931), 127-130; cf. John Wilch, *Ruth* (St. Louis, Missouri: Concordia Publishing House, 2006), 34-35.

[20] Jubilees 6:21; cf. Exodus 23:16; Numbers 28:26. See James Charlesworth, *The Old Testament Pseudepigrapha*, Volume 2 (New York: Doubleday, 1985), 67. See also Jack Sasson, *Ruth* (Sheffield, England: Sheffield Academic Press, 1995), 13.

[21] Genesis 9:1-7 referred to as the "Noahide Laws." Abrahamic Covenant, Genesis 12-16.

[22] Sasson, *Ruth*, 13.

[23] Solomon Zeitlin, "The Book of Jubilees Its Character and Its Significance," *The Jewish Quarterly Review*, 30.1 (July 1939), 3.

[24] It literally means "the counting of the sheaves."

[25] See Leviticus 23:15-16. Solomon Zeitlin, "The Book of Jubilees," 3.

[26] Rabbi A. J. Rosenberg, *The Books of Esther, Song of Songs, Ruth* (New York: The Judaica Press, 1992), xiv.

[27] Sasson, *Ruth*, 13.

[28] John 4:25-26.

Chapter One

[29] NASB.

[30] Judges 2:16-20.

[31] Judges 2:7-14.

[32] F. LaGard Smith, *The Narrated Bible in Chronological Or-*

der (Eugene, Oregon.: Harvest House Publishers, 1999), 343.

[33] Judges 2:16-19.

[34] Judges 19.

[35] Judges 21:6.

[36] In God's great providence the tribe of Benjamin produced Saul (1 Samuel 9:1) and a thousand years later Saul whose name was changed to Paul (Romans 11:1).

[37] 1 Samuel 8:7.

[38] Judges 17:6; 21:25.

[39] K. Lawson Younger, Jr., *Judges, Ruth* (Grand Rapids, Michigan: Zondervan, 2002), 347. See Judges 19.

[40] Ibid., p. 348.

[41] Jack Hillcox, "Harry Vaughn: Neo-Nazi, 18, to Be Sentenced Over Terror Charges," *Sky News*, 12 October 2020, http://news.sky.com/story/harry-vaughan-neo-nazi-18-to-be-sentenced-over-terror-charges-12105837.

[42] Romans 1:25-32, 18; 1 Corinthians 7:2-3; Genesis 1:27-28; Matthew 19:4-6; Leviticus 18:22.

[43] Mohamed K. Jasser, *The Holy Koran: An Interpretative Translation from Classical Arabic into Contemporary English* (Phoenix: Acacia Publishing, Inc.), xiii.

[44] Literally, "in the name of God, the merciful and compassionate."

[45] Lizzie Dearden, "We Must Act Before Another Child Is Killed: Warning Over Abuse Linked to Witchcraft and Possession Beliefs in UK," *Independent*, 19 February 2018, https://www.independent.co.uk/news/uk/crime/witchcraft-posses-sion-child-abuse-murders-warning-figures-spirits-faith-be-

lief-action-call-government-funding-kristy-bamu-a8214196. html.

[46] "Maggie Smythe: 'Monstrous' Man Jailed for Ex-partner's Murder," *BBC News*, September 6, 2019, https://www.bbc.co.uk/ news/uk-england-manchester-49610067.

[47] John 10:10.

[48] Famine caused by drought (Genesis 41:27; 1 Kings 18:2), disease and locust (Amos 4:9-10), warfare (2 Kings 6:24-25; Isaiah 1:7), loss of livestock (1 Kings 18:5).

[49] See Job 42:2.

[50] Genesis 37-50.

[51] Amos 4. See Acts 11:28; Mark 13:8; cf. Haggai 1:10-11; Leviticus 26:18-20; Deuteronomy 28:23-24.

[52] 1 Corinthians 10:11-12; cf. Romans 11:20-22.

[53] Deuteronomy 7:9-10.

[54] 1 John 4:7-8.

[55] 1 Peter 4:7-9 (NLT).

[56] Almighty God (Hebrew).

[57] Luke 11:11-12.

[58] 1 Timothy 6:6.

[59] "Irish Potato Famine," *The History Place*, see http://www. *historyplace.com*/worldhistory/famine/begins.htm as at 8 October 2020.

[60] For more information, see "The Great Famine of 1845," *History Learning Site*, http://www.historylearningsite.co.uk/ ireland_great_famine_of_1845.htm.

[61] James S. Donnelly, *The Great Irish Potato Famine*, (Cheltenham, Gloucester: The History Press, 2002), 20.

[62] Amartya Sen and Jean Drèze, *The Amartya Sen and Jean Drèze Omnibus* (New Delhi, India: Oxford University Press, 1999), 52-56.

[63] Cormac Ó Gráda, *Famine: A Short History* (Princeton: Princeton University Press, Oxford, 2009), 185ff.

[64] Ó Gráda, *Famine*, 190-91.

[65] Ibid.

[66] Genesis 12:3.

[67] See Sasson, *Ruth*, 17.

[68] Robert L. Hubbard, *The Book of Ruth* (Grand Rapids, Michigan: Eerdmans Publishing, 1988), 88; Wilch, *Ruth*, 124; Daniel Block, *Judges, Ruth: An Exegetical and Theological Exposition of Holy Scripture* (Nashville, Tennessee: Broadman & Holman Publishers, 1999), 625; Sasson, *Ruth*, 17.

[69] 1 Chronicles 4:9.

[70] Genesis 38:29.

[71] Genesis 35:18. (Jacob changed his name to *Benjamin* meaning "son of my right hand.")

[72] Sasson, *Ruth*, 18-19.

[73] Genesis 35:19, 48:7; Ruth 4:11; Micah 5:2.

[74] Joshua 19:15.

[75] 1 Chronicles 2:19, 50-51, 4:4. See Hubbard, *The Book of Ruth*, 91.

[76] Micah 5:2.

[77] Genesis 35:19; cf. 48:7.

[78] Jacob Neusner, *Ruth Rabbah: An Analytical Translation, Brown Judaic Study 183* (Atlanta: Scholars Press, 1983) 47.

[79] See Deuteronomy 23:4; Judges 11:17.

[80] Deuteronomy 11:12-17.

[81] Block, Judges, Ruth, 627.

[82] Sasson proposes the likelihood that the setting of Ruth may have been the period between Ehud and Jephthah, except for the brief reign of Eglon, then Moab would either have been ruled by Israel or "fell within its sphere of influence." Sasson, *Ruth,* 15.

[83] Genesis 12:10-20.

[84] Genesis 26:1-5.

[85] Hebrews 10:18.

[86] Genesis 12:15-20.

[87] Genesis 12:10-13; 17–20.

[88] Genesis 20:1-4.

[89] Genesis 20:14-18.

[90] Genesis 26:1-11.

[91] 2 Kings 8:1.

[92] Psalm 103; Numbers 14:18.

[93] Romans 10:17; Hebrews 11:6.

[94] Genesis 21:5. The promise was made when Abraham was 75 years old.

[95] 1 John 1:8-10, see also 1 John 2:1-6.

[96] John 8:10-11; see also John 5:14.

[97] Romans 1:21-24; 2 Corinthians 4:4.

[98] Romans 1:26-32.

[99] Hebrews 11:1.

[100] Deuteronomy 8:3.

[101] Genesis 37:25-28.

[102] Genesis 41:37-46.

[103] Daniel 3:27; 6:21.

[104] Hebrews 13:8; Isaiah 43:12; Psalm 66:12.

[105] 1 Corinthians 1:27.

[106] Grapes would be normally trodden in a winepress, which was a circular pit carved into a rock.

[107] Judges 6:19-21.

[108] Judges 6:36-40.

[109] Deuteronomy 6:16.

[110] Judges 7:12.

[111] Judges 7:19-25.

[112] John 20:31.

[113] Zechariah 4:6.

[114] Genesis 19:30-38.

[115] Deuteronomy 23:2-3.

[116] Deuteronomy 23:4.

[117] Numbers 25:1-2.

[118] Numbers 22-24.

[119] 1 Samuel 22:3.

[120] Neusner, *Ruth Rabbah*, 60; cf. Block, *Judges, Ruth*, 628.

[121] Genesis 17:15-16; 21:1-5.

[122] Genesis 25: 21-26.

[123] 1 Samuel 1:20. Hannah bore three sons and two daughters (1 Samuel 2:21).

[124] Ruth 1:5.

[125] Psalm 30:5, Isaiah 25:8.

[126] 2 Corinthians 1:3-4; Hebrews 12:10-11.

[127] John 11:25; Revelation 21:4; 1 Corinthians 15:55.

[128] Revelation 21:4.

[129] "Alpha Talks," *HTB Church Online*, https://www.htb.org/alpha-talks.

[130] Galatians 5:16-25.

[131] Donald Barnhouse, *Genesis: A Devotional Commentary*, Vol. 2 (Grand Rapids: Zondervan, 1973), 81.

[132] John 8:32.

[133] Cf. Frederic Bush, *Word Biblical Commentary: Ruth-Esther* (Colombia: Nelson, 1996), 68.

[134] Phyllis Trible, *God and the Rhetoric of Sexuality* (Philadelphia: Fortress, 1978), 167-68.

[135] See Hals, *The Theology of the Book of Ruth*, 6.

[136] Sir John Hawkins, a contemporary of Handel's who wrote music history. See Marian Van Til, *George Frideric Handel: A Music Lover's Guide to His Life, His Faith and the Development of Messiah* (Youngstown, New York: WordPower Publishing, 2007), 278.

[137] There has been speculation that it could have been a stroke or muscular disorder.

[138] Patrick Kavanaugh, *Spiritual Lives of the Great Composers* (Grand Rapids: Zondervan, 1966), 29.

[139] The words to an opera.

[140] The Messiah presents the entire gospel relating to salvation history, from Old Testament prophecies of the coming Messiah to their fulfilment in the New Testament, in the birth of Christ, His death and resurrection, and His eternal reign.

[141] 2 Corinthians 12:2. See Kavanaugh, *Spiritual Lives of the Great Composers*, 30.

[142] See Marian Van Til, *George Frideric Handel: A Music Lover's Guide*, 268-70.

[143] Op cit., p.12, referencing Charles Burney, on Charity and Messiah: "An Account of the Musical Performances in Westminster Abbey, and the Pantheon, in Commemoration of Handel," *A Sketch of the Life of Handel*, 27.

[144] Kavanaugh, *Spiritual Lives of the Great Composers*, 31, referencing Percy M. Young, *The Oratorios of Handel*, (London: Dobson Ltd., 1949), 100.

[145] The Foundling Hospital was not restricted to medical facilities. It was a charity that provided a home for babies born out of wedlock (mothers of good reputation) or abandoned. They were then found foster homes, and when they were four or five years old, they were returned to Foundling to be educated. At adolescence they were trained: the boys for the army, and the girls became ladies' maids.

[146] See Van Til, George Frideric Handel: *A Music Lover's Guide*, 317, referencing Charles Burney, *Sketch of the Life of Handel*, 31.

[147] Job 19:25.

[148] Born in Leicestershire, 24 August 1707–17 June 1791. An aristocrat by birth, she married Theophilus Hastings, the ninth Earl of Huntingdon.

[149] Aaron Seymour published anonymously a two-volume hagiographical work in 1839.

[150] Adapted from Faith Cook, *Selina: Countess of Huntingdon* (Edinburgh: Banner of Truth Trust, 2001); Carol Gwynne, "The Issue and Consequence of Suffering" (Thesis M.A. 2007).

[151] Romans 8:28.

[152] See Hebrews 11, commonly known as the "Hall of Faith."

The names mentioned, were people whom the world would consider as unworthy—but they all had faith and conquered kingdoms.

[153] James 1:2.

[154] Pronounced *pi-ras-mos*.

[155] Acts 16:22-35.

[156] James 1:4.

[157] Greg Harris, *The Cup and the Glory* (The Woodlands, Texas: Kress Christian Publications, 2006), 121.

[158] Ibid.

[159] Psalm 94:14.

[160] Deuteronomy10:18. See also Isaiah 41:1.

[161] Luke 8:2.

[162] Mark 16:9, John 20:11-16.

[163] John 4:11-26, 39.

[164] John 11:17, 38-43.

[165] Luke 23:49.

[166] Luke 10:39-42; John 14, 15, 17; 1 Corinthians 2:13; Romans 5:5; Ephesians 3:16.

[167] *Strong's Concordance*, 3899.

[168] Hubbard, *The Book of Ruth*, 100.

[169] Genesis 40:4.

[170] Jeremiah 25:12; see *Strong's Concordance*, Hebrew 6485, *paqad*.

[171] Luke 1:67-68.

[172] John 6:33-35, 48.

[173] Craig R. Koester, *Symbolism in the Fourth Gospel: Meaning, Mystery, Community*, 27.

174 John 6:27-29.

175 John 6:35.

176 John 10:10.

177 See *Strong's Concordance* 2222.

178 Amos 8:11.

179 2 Samuel 12:20-23.

180 Ezra 9:6-8.

181 John 14:16-17,26; 15:26; Romans 8:2.

182 John 16:33.

183 Greek meaning "life"; John 1:4; 6:35; 10:10.

184 Genesis 18:1.

185 Genesis 18:10, 21:2, 5.

186 Genesis13:12-13; 18:20.

187 Genesis 19:24.

188 God did not appear in physical form to Abraham. See Exodus 33:23, Deuteronomy 4:15. The burning bush of Exodus 3:2-3 was a physical representation of God's presence. For detailed information see John H. Sailhamer, *The Expositor's Bible Commentary: Genesis* (Zondervan, 2017), 144-151.

189 Author's insert.

190 Arthur E. Cundall and Leon Morris, *Judges and Ruth* (Leicester, England; IVP, 1968), 254.

191 Ruth 1:21.

192 Acts 12:6-11.

193 Romans 5:12; Genesis 3.

194 John 14:18; Deuteronomy 31:6; Hebrews 13:5; James 1:2-4

195 Ruth 3:3-4.

196 Ruth 1:8.

[197] Genesis 38:11; Leviticus 22:13; Numbers 30:16; Deuteronomy 22:21; Judges 19:2-3.

[198] Genesis 24:28.

[199] In her time some 80 years ago, particularly in the Eastern culture, women had a tertiary education if they were fortunate. Their role in society was to marry at the age of sixteen and breed children! If they were fortunate enough and married well, they would have a retinue of servants to meet their every need.

[200] Exodus 22:22.

[201] Deuteronomy 14:29; 16:11. See also Isaiah 1:17-23; 10:1-2; Jeremiah 7:4-7; 22:3; Lamentations 5:2-3; Proverbs 14:31; 22:9, 22-23; Malachi 3:5.

[202] John 4:4-42.

[203] Acts 6:1.

[204] Acts 6:1, 9:36-43.

[205] 1 Timothy 5:3-16.

[206] Most scholars are of the opinion that by the time Jesus attained adulthood, His mother Mary was a widow.

[207] John 19:30.

[208] John 19:27; Jesus' cry of "It is finished!" was triumphant. His mission was accomplished He was afflicted for our sins that we may receive grace, mercy and eternal life. See Isaiah 53.

[209] John 14:16-18.

[210] Jeremiah 29:11.

[211] As in the Lord's Prayer.

[212] Ruth 1:8b.

[213] 2 Samuel 15:20.

[214] 2 Samuel 15:21.

215 2 Samuel 2:5-6.

216 Genesis 24:12.

217 Ephesians 1:11; Romans 8:17; Galatians 4:4.

218 Ruth 1:9.

219 See Wilch, *Ruth*, 135.

220 Ruth 1:12.

221 Ruth 1:13.

222 Bush, Ruth–Esther, 86.

223 Micah 7:18-19; Daniel 9:9; Ephesians 1:7.

224 Isaiah 53:5; Romans 3:23; 1 Peter 2:24.

225 *Strong's* 3986.

226 Revelation 3:20.

227 Genesis 31:55.

228 1 Samuel 20:41.

229 Acts 20:37-38.

230 See James 3:6-9.

231 1 Samuel 17.

232 Neusner, *Ruth Rabbah*, 77; See 2 Samuel 21:22.

233 Ruth 1:8.

234 Matthew 6:6; Ecclesiastes 4:12.

235 Numbers 21:29; Jeremiah 48:13, 35; Leviticus 20:1-5; Jeremiah 48:7, 13, 46; 1 Kings 11:7, 33; 2 Kings 3:27, 16:2-3, 21:6, 23:13; Ezekiel 20:30-34, 23:37. Of interest, see http://ancienthistory.about.com/od/cgodsandgoddesses/a/chemosh.htm.

236 According to Midrashic writings, Ruth and Orpah were the daughters of Eglon, king of Moab.

237 1 Samuel 22:3-4. David's father Jesse was married to an Israelite named Nizbet. The Bible does not name his moth-

er, but the Babylonian Talmud does (Baba Batra 91A). Jacob Neusner, Tzvee Zahavy (ed.), *Babylonian Talmud: A Translation and Commentary* (Peabody, Massachusetts: Hendrickson Publisher, Inc., 2007).

[238] *Strong's* 1692.

[239] King James Version. Jesus Christ re-emphasised this principle in Matthew 19:3-9.

[240] Block, Judges-Ruth, 640.

[241] Wilch, *Ruth*, 170; Romans 12:12.

[242] Wilch, *Ruth*, 171; Hubbard, *Ruth*, 120; Block, *Judges-Ruth*, 641.

[243] Romans 11:17.

[244] Genesis 25:8; 35:29.

[245] Genesis 49:29-32; 50:12-13. See also Deuteronomy 32:50; Judges 2:10; 1 Kings 2:10, 11:43, 14:31.

[246] Trible, *God and the Rhetoric of Sexuality*, 173.

[247] Jeremiah 18-20.

[248] 1 Timothy 2:4.

[249] Luke 8:14.

[250] Luke 8:15.

[251] Psalm 86:15; 103:8-10; 145:8-9.

[252] Isaiah 1:18-19 (NIV).

[253] Matthew 7:9-11; Luke 11:11-13 (NIV).

[254] James 2:2-4, 9.

[255] Galatians 3:28.

[256] Ephesians 6:2.

[257] Ecclesiastes 4:12; 1 Peter 3:8; Romans 12:16; Hebrews 12:14.

[258] Genesis 2:24; Matthew 19:5; Mark 10:8; Ephesians 5:31.

[259] Hubbard, *The Book of Ruth*, 123-24.

[260] James 2:14.

[261] Isaiah 1:17, 58:10; Matthew 10:42

[262] See Block, *Judges, Ruth*, 605-606; cf. Cundall and Morris, Judges and Ruth, 254.

[263] Isaiah 55:6-9.

[264] Block, *Judges Ruth*, 647. See Exodus 34:6; Psalm 103:8; James 5:11.

[265] Bush, *Ruth-Esther*, 95-96, seems to be quoting Trible, 173.

[266] Psalm 94:19; 145:19; John 15:7, 16.

[267] Matthew 11:29.

[268] Philippians 4:7.

[269] John 16:13.

[270] Deuteronomy 31:8.

[271] Jeremiah 1:5; Psalm 139:13.

[272] See Edward Campbell, Jr., "The Hebrew Short Story: A Study of Ruth" in *A Light Unto My Path*, 98.

[273] Klaas A.D. Smelik, *Writings From Ancient Israel: A Handbook of Historical and Religious Documents*. Translated by G. I. Davies (Edinburgh, Scotland: T&T Clark, 1991), 21-22. Robert A. S. Macalister, *The Excavation of Gezer: 1902-1905 and 1907-1909*, Reprint Cornell University Library, Columbia University Libraries and the New York Public Library, 1999, 22-27.

[274] Victor H. Matthews, *A Brief History of Ancient Israel* (Louisville, Kentucky: Westminster John Knox Press, 2002), 38.

[275] Jubilees 6:21, cf. Exodus 23:16; Numbers 28:26, See Charlesworth, *The Old Testament Pseudepigrapha*, 67.

[276] Zeitlin, "The Book of Jubilees," *The Jewish Quarterly Review*, 6-7; cf. Charlesworth, *The Old Testament Pseudepigrapha*, 67.

[277] Genesis, Exodus, Leviticus, Numbers and Deuteronomy. Also known as the first five books of Moses.

[278] Derived from the Hebrew word "to teach" and refers to five Books of the Pentateuch. Sometimes also referred to as Chumash (Hebrew five). There is also an Oral Torah developed by the rabbis, and this oral tradition was passed down and eventually written in the Mishnah and the Talmud.

[279] Also known as Pentecost by the Hellenistic Jews.

[280] Jubilees 6:21; Exodus 23.

[281] Third month of the Jewish year—Western correlation 15 May–14 June, which was the time of the wheat harvest.

[282] Zeitlin, "The Book of Jubilees," *The Jewish Quarterly Review*, 3.

[283] Leviticus 23:15-21.

[284] Leviticus 23:10 (NASB): *"Speak to the sons of Israel and say to them, 'When you enter the land which I am going to give to you and reap its harvest, then you shall bring in the sheaf of the first fruits of your harvest to the priest.'"*

[285] Exodus 23:16; Numbers 28:26.

[286] English trans. Pentecost.

[287] Sasson, *Ruth*, 12; cf. Rabbi Rosenberg, *Esther, Song of Songs, Ruth*, xiv.

[288] Rabbi Rosenberg, *Esther, Song of Songs, Ruth*, xiv.

[289] John 7:5, 10.

[290] Exodus 17.

[291] John 7:37-38.

[292] John 7:39.

[293] Acts 2:1-4.

[294] Acts 1:3.

---

[295] Acts 1:4-5.

Chapter Two

[296] NASB.

[297] Psalm 82:3; Isaiah 1:17; Deuteronomy 24:19-21; Leviticus 19:9, 23:22.

[298] Dr. Nell Darby, "Gleaning, poor women, and the law," http://www.criminal historian.com/ gleaning-poor-women-and-the-law/. See also Stephen Hussey, "The Last Survivor of an Ancient Race: The Changing Face of Essex Gleaning," http://www.bahs. org.uk/AGHR/ARTICLES/45n1a5.pdf.

[299] Matthew 25:35-44.

[300] JPS Tanakh 1917.

[301] Ruth 4:1.

[302] See 1 Corinthians 12:4-11.

[303] 1 Corinthians 12:12-26.

[304] The end of the wheat harvest in late May coincides with Pentecost.

[305] Ruth 2:9-10.

[306] Ruth 2:2. See also 2:22.

[307] Bruce K. Waltke, *An Old Testament Theology* (Grand Rapids: Zondervan, 2007), 855.

[308] 2 Corinthians 12:9.

[309] Deuteronomy 19:9. (See also Deuteronomy 8:6, Romans 13:13, Ephesians 2:10.)

[310] Zechariah 3:7.

[311] Genesis 39:2-6; Psalm 1:1-3, 37:4; Proverbs 16:3; Philippians 4:13.

---

[312] Ruth 2:3.

[313] See Bush, *Ruth-Esther*, 248.

[314] Cf. Amos 3:6; Lamentations 3:37-38; Isaiah 45:1-8; Block, *Judges, Ruth*, 653.

[315] Younger, Jr., *Judges, Ruth*, 441.

[316] Kirsten Nielsen, *Ruth* (Louisville, Ky,: Westminster John Knox Press, 1997), 41; cf. Hubbard, *The Book of Ruth*, 141; Younger, Jr., *Judges, Ruth*, 441; Block, *Judges, Ruth*, 653.

[317] Hals, *The Theology of the Book of Ruth*, 11-12.

[318] Ecclesiastes 9:1-2.

[319] Exodus 20:17.

[320] Hebrews 13:5; Philippians 4:6-7; 1 Peter 5:7; Deuteronomy 31:6.

[321] John 10:10.

[322] John 16:13; Galatians 5:25.

[323] 2 Timothy 3:16.

[324] Luke 6:38.

[325] Leviticus 19:9; 23:22.

[326] Psalm 84:11.

[327] Numbers 6:24; Deuteronomy 28:8; 2 Chronicles 15:2; cf. Luke 1:28; 1 Thessalonians 3:12; 2 Timothy 4:22.

[328] Bush, *Ruth-Esther*, 113.

[329] Ruth 2:7.

[330] Ruth 3:11.

[331] Genesis 24:13, 18, 20; 1 Samuel 9:11; Foreigners to draw water, Joshua 9:21, 27; cf. John 4:7.

[332] Ruth 2:2.

[333] See Luke 2:52: "*Jesus increased in wisdom and stature and*

in favour with God and man."

[334] See James 2:14-22.

[335] Psalm 91:4.

[336] Hebrews 11.

[337] An underlying reality.

[338] John Chrysostom, *Nicene and Post-Nicene Fathers,* (First Series, vol. 14), 462-64 cited in James D. Smith III, *The Challenge of Bible Translation: Essays in Honor of Ronald F. Youngblood,* Edited by Glen G. Scorgie, Mark L. Strauss and Steven M. Voth (Grand Rapids: Zondervan, 2003), 383.

[339] Philippians 2:3-4.

[340] Jeremiah 29:11.

[341] Deuteronomy 28:13.

[342] Ruth 3:3.

[343] Luke 21:1-4.

[344] Luke 6:27-36.

[345] Luke 6:38.

[346] Author's insert.

[347] Philippians 2:3-8.

[348] Edward Campbell, *Ruth* (New York: Doubleday & Company, Inc, 1975), 104.

[349] See Campbell, *Ruth,* 241.

[350] Hals, *The Theology of the Book of Ruth,* 16.

[351] John 16:13.

[352] 2 Chronicles 16:9.

[353] Judges 6.

[354] Genesis 40:1-20.

[355] Genesis 41.

Chapter Three

356 Hebrew "find rest" (Ruth 1:9).

357 *Kanaph* can also mean "corners of garment or skirt."

358 NASB.

359 Deuteronomy 16:13.

360 Hosea 9:1 (New Living Translation).

361 Leviticus 25:23.

362 Micah 4:12 (NLT).

363 Psalm 1:4.

364 Leviticus 26:3-10.

365 Joel 2:24-25.

366 Matthew 3:11; Luke 3:17.

367 Hessian is a woven rough cloth made from jute or hemp.

368 2 Samuel 14:2.

369 Genesis 38:14.

370 Genesis 38:27-30.

371 Genesis 38:9.

372 Genesis 38:24-26.

373 *Perez* means "breach."

374 Some scholars have suggested that Ruth was told to uncover the lower half of Boaz, not just his feet, and it was there close to his body that she lay. See Bush, *Ruth-Esther*, 152.

375 Genesis19:30-38. The elder daughter named her son Moab, and the younger named her son *Ben-Ammi* who became the father of the Ammonites.

376 Ruth 1:16-17.

377 Ruth 2:4, 12.

378 Genesis 19:30-38.

379 2 Samuel 11:4.

380 Stephen Gabriel Rosenberg, *Esther, Ruth, Jonah Deciphered* (Israel: Devora Publishing Company, 2004), 121; Rabbi Meir Zlotowitz, comp., *Megillas Ruth* (New York: Mesorah Publications, Ltd, 1976), 86.

381 Block, *Judges, Ruth*, 686; Sasson, *Ruth*, 70.

382 Exodus 11:4; 12:23-29; Judges 16:3; Job 34:20.

383 *Shivered* or *startled* in 3:8.

384 Sasson, *Ruth*, 78-80; cf. Kirsten Nielsen, *Ruth*, 72.

385 Ariola Pelaia, "The Legend of Lilith," April 16, 2019, *Learn Religions*, https://www.thoughtco.com/legend-of-lilith-origins-2076660.

386 Rabbi Jill Hammer, "Lilith: Lady Flying in Darkness," *Jewish Learning*, https://www.myjewishlearning.com/article/lilith-lady-flying-in-darkness/; also https://www.coursehero.com/ file/ p605v6vd/in-the-renaissance-Michelangelo-portrayed-her-as-a-half-woman-half-serpent/.

387 "Lilith," *Bible History Daily*, https://www.biblicalarchaeology.org/daily/people-cultures-in-the-bible/people-in-the-bible/lilith/.

388 Genesis 39:6-16.

389 Ruth 3:4.

390 Ruth 3:9.

391 Translation NASB. In the NIV: *"Take your maidservant under your wing."*

392 According to *Collins Dictionary*—"to submit, to dwell, continuously remain, to comply"

393 Psalm 36:7.

[394] Psalm 17:8.

[395] Psalm 57:1.

[396] Psalm 63:7.

[397] Psalm 46:1.

[398] Luke 13:34.

[399] Nehemiah 13:23-31.

[400] Matheson, *Teach Me Your Paths*, 227; cf. Hubbard, *The Book of Ruth*, 41.

[401] Genesis 2:23.

[402] 1 Corinthians 6:9-11; 1 Thessalonians 4:3-4.

[403] Colossians 1:13; Acts 26:18.

[404] Romans 10:9-10; 1 John 1:19.

[405] John 3:16.

[406] Isaiah 43:25; Micah 7:19; Luke 24:46-47.

[407] John 8:32.

[408] Ruth 3:3.

[409] "...*let us not love in word or talk but in deed and in truth*" (1 John 3:18).

[410] Matthew 5:16; cf 13.

[411] Ruth 3:10.

[412] Ruth 2:20.

[413] Ruth 2:11-12.

[414] Block, *Judges, Ruth*, 692.

[415] Hubbard, *The Book of Ruth*, 215.

[416] Ecclesiastes 3:13; 1 Corinthians 3:7; Ephesians 2:8. See also Wilch, *Ruth*, 70; cf. Hals, *The Theology of the Book of Ruth*, 10.

[417] Ruth 2:11-12.

[418] Ruth 3:10.

[419] "Boaz was eighty years old and had not been visited with child...Ruth was forty years old...." Neusner, *Ruth Rabbah*, 155; Rabbi Zlotowitz, *Megillas Ruth*, 121. See Sasson, *Ruth*, 86; Katherine Doob Sakenfeld, *Ruth*, (Louisville, Ky.: John Knox Press, 1999), 79.

[420] Ruth 3:11.

[421] "your people...my God" recalls the covenant promise "I will be your God, and you shall be my people" Genesis 17:7-8; Exodus 6:7; Deuteronomy 29:13; Jeremiah 24:7, 31:33; Hosea 2:23; Zechariah 8:8; 2 Corinthians 6:16; Revelation 21:7.

[422] Judges 2:16; Judges 4 and 5.

[423] Judges 4:18-21; 5:24-27.

[424] 2 Kings 22.

[425] Not to be confused with Mary of Bethany, a sinful woman who anointed Jesus and wiped His feet with her hair (Luke 7:36-38).

[426] Luke 8:1-3.

[427] Acts 12:12.

[428] 1 Corinthians 1:11.

[429] Colossians 4:15. Note Nymphas is to be read as Nympha, designating a woman.

[430] Ruth 3:17.

[431] Campbell, *A Light Unto My Path*, 98.

Chapter Four

[432] NASB.

[433] Deuteronomy 21:18-21.

[434] Genesis 19:1.

[435] 2 Samuel 18:1-4.

[436] 2 Samuel 18:24, 33.

[437] 2 Samuel 19:7-8.

[438] Proverbs 8:3-5; 1:21.

[439] John 10:14.

[440] John 10:3, 7.

[441] See Bush, *Ruth/Esther*, 197-99 for a more detailed account.

[442] Ruth 2:20.

[443] Ruth 3:9.

[444] Robert Gordis, "Love, Marriage, and Business in the Book of Ruth" in *A Light unto My Path, Old Testament Studies in Honour of Jacob M. Myers*, ed. Howard N. Bream, Ralph D. Heim, Carey A. Moore (Philadelphia: Temple University Press, 1974), 246; Hubbard, *The Book of Ruth*, 51.

[445] Translation: "hidden, nameless."

[446] Ruth 4:5.

[447] Ruth 4:6.

[448] Rabbi Zlotowitz, *Megillas Ruth*, 121, 125.

[449] Ruth 4:7-8. As suggested by Rav Alkabetz, it was a custom that "fell into disuse for some time, and Boaz reinstituted it on that occasion." Rabbi Zlotowitz, *Megillas Ruth*, 127; cf. Gordis, *A Light unto My Path*, 255, 258.

[450] Cf. Leviticus 25:25.

[451] Ruth 4:10.

[452] Although the narrative does not state precisely how long she was married to Mahlon, one can presume from 1:4 that it could have been for ten years.

[453] Ruth 2:10.

[454] Block, *Judges, Ruth*, 725; Hubbard, *The Book of Ruth*, 256.

[455] Ruth 1:8-9.

[456] Campbell, *A Light unto My Path*, 97.

[457] John 3:16.

[458] John 10:10.

[459] Philippians 2:3-4.

[460] Genesis 28:1-2.

[461] Genesis 29:31, 30:22.

[462] Genesis 35:23.

[463] Genesis 29:30, 35:16-18.

[464] Psalm 89:4.

[465] Genesis 3:15; cf. Hebrews 3:6.

[466] Matthew 1:6-16; cf. Luke 3:23-31.

[467] Psalm 91.

[468] Ruth 4:15.

[469] Meaning "servant or workman."

[470] Ruth 4:11.

[471] Matthew 1:5,16; cf. 1Chronicles 2:5-16.

[472] Matthew 1:16.

[473] Genesis 38:26.

[474] Joshua 2:12-17.

[475] Hebrews 11:31.

[476] 2 Samuel 11.

[477] 1 Kings 11:17.

[478] Ruth 4:16 (NJKV). Alternative ESV translation: "*Then Naomi took the child and laid him on her lap and became his nurse.*"

[479] Pronounced "aw man." See *Strong's* 0539.

[480] Proverbs11:24-25.

Epilogue

[481] Nathan Stone, *Names of God* (Chicago: Moody Press, 1944), 32.

[482] Thomas R. Schreiner, *New Testament Theology, Magnifying God in Christ* (Grand Rapids: Baker Academic, 2008), 349.

[483] James Dunn, *The Theology of Paul the Apostle* (Edinburgh, Scotland: T&T Clark, 1998), 317.

[484] Ibid., 317-18.

[485] 2 Chronicles 7:14.

[486] Philippians 3:5-6.

[487] Acts 7:54-60, 8:1.

[488] Acts 8:3.

[489] 1 Corinthians 15:9.

[490] Acts 9:1-19.

[491] See F. F. Bruce, *Paul, Apostle of the Heart Set Free* (Carlisle, Cumbria: The Paternoster Press Ltd., 2000) 320-27.

[492] 2 Kings 21:3; 2 Chronicles 33:3.

[493] 2 Chronicles 33:10-13.

[494] Ephesians 2:8-9.

[495] 2 Chronicles 7:13-14 (NKJV).

The Book of Ruth
Works Cited

Auld, A. Graeme. *Joshua, Judges, and Ruth.* Louisville, Kentucky: Westminster John Knox Press, 1984.

Baab, Otto J. *The Theology of the Old Testament.* Nashville, Tennessee: Abingdon Press, 1931.

Barnhouse, Donald. *Genesis: A Devotional Commentary,* Vol. 2. Grand Rapids, Michigan: Zondervan, 1973.

Block, Daniel. *Judges, Ruth: An Exegetical and Theological Exposition of Holy Scripture.* Nashville: Broadman & Holman Publishers, 1999.

Brown, Raymond E. *The Birth of the Messiah.* New York: Doubleday, 1993.

Bruce, F. F. *Paul, Apostle of the Heart Set Free.* Carlisle, Cumbria: The Paternoster Press Ltd., 2000.

Bush, Frederic. *Word Biblical Commentary: Ruth-Esther.* Colombia: Nelson Reference & Electronic, 1996.

Campbell, Edward. *Ruth.* New York: Doubleday & Company, Inc, 1975.

Campbell, Jr., Edward. "The Hebrew Short Story: A Study of Ruth" in *A Light unto My Path: Old Testament Studies in Honor of Jacob M. Myers.* Ed. by Howard N. Bream, Ralph D. Heim, Carey A. Moore. Philadelphia: Temple University Press, 1974.

Charlesworth, James H. (ed.). *The Old Testament Pseudepigrapha*, Volume 2 of 2. New York: Doubleday, 1985.

Cook, Faith. *Selina: Countess of Huntingdon*. Edinburgh: Banner of Truth Trust, 2001.

Cundall, Arthur E. and Leon Morris. *Judges and Ruth*. Leicester, England: Inter-Varsity Press, 1968.

Darby, Dr. Nell. "Gleaning, poor women, and the law." http://www.criminal historian.com/ gleaning-poor-women-and-the-law.

Dearden, Lizzie. "We Must Act Before Another Child Is Killed: Warning Over Abuse Linked to Witchcraft and Possession Beliefs in UK," *Independent*, 19 February 2018, https://www.independent.co.uk/news/uk/crime/witchcraft-possession-child-abuse-murders-warning-figures-spirits-faith-belief-action-call-government-funding-kristy-bamu-a8214196.html.

Donnelly, James S. *The Great Irish Potato Famine*. Cheltenham, Gloucestershire: The History Press, 2002.

Dunn, James. *The Theology of Paul the Apostle*. Edinburgh, Scotland: T&T Clark, 1998.

Fewell, Danna Nolan. *Compromising Redemption: Relating Characters in the Book of Ruth*. Louisville: Westminster John Knox Press, 1990.

Gordis, Robert. "Love, Marriage, and Business in the Book of Ruth" in *A Light unto My Path, Old Testament Studies in Honor of Jacob M. Myers*. Ed. by Howard N. Bream, Ralph D. Heim, Carey A. Moore. Philadelphia: Temple University Press, 1974.

Gráda, Cormac Ó. *Famine: A Short History*. Oxfordshire: Princeton University Press, 2009.

Gwynne, Carol. "The Issue and Consequence of Suffering." Thesis M.A., 2007.

Hals, Ronald M. *The Theology of the Book of Ruth*. Philadelphia: Fortress Press, 1969.

Hammer, Rabbi Jill. "Lilith: Lady Flying in Darkness." *Jewish Learning*. https://www.myjewishlearning.com/article/lilith-lady-flying-in-darkness/

Harris, Greg. *The Cup and the Glory*. The Woodlands, Texas: Kress Christian Publications, 2006.

Hillcox, Jack. "Harry Vaughn: Neo-Nazi, 18, to Be Sentenced Over Terror Charges." *Sky News,* 12 October 2020, http://news.sky.com/story/harry-vaughan-neo-nazi-18-to-be-sentenced-over-terror-charges-12105837.

Hubbard, Robert L. *The Book of Ruth*. Grand Rapids: Eerdmans Publishing, 1988.

Hussey, Stephen. "The Last Survivor of an Ancient Race: The Changing Face of Essex Gleaning," http://www.bahs.org.uk/AGHR/ARTICLES/45n1a5.pdf.

"Irish Potato Famine," *The History Place*, see http://www.historyplace.com/ world history/ famine/begins.htm.

Jasser, Mohamed K. *The Holy Koran: An Interpretative Translation from Classical Arabic into Contemporary English*. Phoenix, Arizona: Acacia Publishing, Inc., 1985.

Josephus. *Josephus: The Complete Works*. Trans. by A.M. William Whiston. Nashville: Thomas Nelson Publishers, 1998.

Kavanaugh, Patrick. *Spiritual Lives of the Great Composers*. Grand Rapids: Zondervan, 1966.

Koester, Craig. *Symbolism in the Fourth Gospel: Meaning, Mys-*

tery, Community. Philadelphia, Pennsylvania: Fortress Press, 2003.

Liefeld, Walter L. *The Expositor's Bible Commentary: Matthew, Mark, Luke*. Grand Rapids: Zondervan Publishing House, 1984.

Loader, J.A. "Of Barley, Bulls, Land, and Levirate," in *Studies in Deuteronomy in Honour of S. J. Labuschagne on the Occasion of His Sixty-fifth Birthday*. New York: Brill, 1994.

Macalister, Robert A. S. The Excavation of Gezer: 1902-1905 and 1907-1909. Reprint Cornell University Library, Columbia University Libraries and the New York Public Library, 1999.

"Maggie Smythe: 'Monstrous' Man Jailed for Ex-partner's Murder," *BBC News*, September 6, 2019, https://www.bbc.co.uk/news/uk-england-manchester-49610067.

Matheson, Roy R., "The Hebrew Short Story: A Study of Ruth" *Teach Me Your Paths: Studies in Old Testament Literature and Theology*. Edited by John Kessler and Jeffrey Greenman. Toronto: Clements Publishing, 2001.

Matthews, Victor H. *A Brief History of Ancient Israel*. Louisville: Westminster John Knox Press, 2002.

Neusner, Jacob, Ed., *The Babylonian Talmud: A Translation and Commentary*. Peabody, Mass.: Hendrickson Publisher, Inc., 2007.

Neusner, Jacob. *Ruth Rabbah: An Analytical Translation*. Atlanta, Georgia.: Scholars Press, 1989.

Nielsen, Kirsten. *Ruth*. Louisville, Kentucky.: Westminster John Knox Press, 1997.

Pelaia, Ariola. "The Legend of Lilith," April 16, 2019. *Learn Religions.* https://www.thoughtco.com/legend-of-lilith-origins-2076660.

Rosenberg, Rabbi A. J. *The Books of Esther, Song of Songs, Ruth.* New York: The Judaica Press, 1992.

Rosenberg, Stephen Gabriel. *Esther, Ruth, Jonah Deciphered: The Complete Hebrew Text with a New Historical Commentary.* Israel: Devora Publishing Company, 2004.

Sailhamer, John H. *The Expositor's Bible Commentary: Genesis.* Grand Rapids: Zondervan, 2017.

Sakenfeld, Katherine Doob. *Ruth Interpretation: A Bible Commentary for Teaching & Preaching.* Louisville: John Knox Press, 1999.

Sasson, Jack M. *Ruth: A New Translation with a Philological Commentary and a Formalist-folklorist Interpretation.* Sheffield, England: Sheffield Academic Press, 1989 Reprint 1995).

Schreiner, Thomas R. *New Testament Theology, Magnifying God in Christ.* Grand Rapids: Baker Academic, 2008.

Sen, Amartya and Jean Drèze. *The Amartya Sen and Jean Drèze Omnibus.* New Delhi, India: Oxford University Press, 1999.

Smelik, Klaas A. D. *Writings from Ancient Israel: A Handbook of Historical and Religious Documents.* Translated by G. I. Davies. Edinburgh, Scotland: T&T Clark, 1991.

Smith III, James D. *The Challenge of Bible Translation: Essays in Honor of Ronald F. Youngblood.* Ed. by. Glen G. Scorgie, et al. Grand Rapids: Zondervan, 2003.

Smith, F. LaGard. *The Narrated Bible in Chronological Order.* Eugene, Oregon: Harvest House Publishers, 1999.

Stone, Nathan. *Names of God.* Chicago: Moody Press, 1944.

Strong, James. *Strong's Exhaustive Concordance.* Tulsa, Oklahoma: American College Press, 1940.

Trible, Phyllis. *God and the Rhetoric of Sexuality.* Philadelphia: Fortress Press, 1978.

Trueman, C. N. "The Great Famine of 1845." *History Learning Site.* 29 October 2020, http://www.historylearningsite.co.uk/ireland_great_famine_of_1845.htm.

Van Til, Marian. *George Frideric Handel: A Music Lover's Guide to His Life, His Faith and the Development of Messiah.* Youngstown, New York: WordPower Publishing, 2007.

Waltke, Bruce K. *An Old Testament Theology.* Grand Rapids: Zondervan, 2007.

Wilch, John. *Ruth* (Concordia Commentary). St. Louis: Concordia Publishing House, 2006.

Younger, Jr., K. Lawson. *Judges, Ruth* (The NIV Application Commentary). Grand Rapids: Zondervan, 2002.

Zeitlin, Solomon. "The Book of Jubilees: Its Character and Its Significance." *The Jewish Quarterly Review.* 30, no. 1. July 1939.

Zlotowitz, Rabbi Meir, Trans. *The Book of Ruth: Megillas Ruth.* New York: Mesorah Publications, Ltd., 1976.

About the Author

For the past 28 years, Dr. Carol Gwynne has used her knowledge and skills to counsel the needy, both within and without the Church, in gratitude to God for turning her life around from one of total chaos, to a life of peace and fulfilment.

In 1992, this author completed a Christian Counselling course at Waverley Abbey, and was mentored for a brief period by the late Selwyn Hughes, who made an enormous impact on her life.

Thereon her pursuit of biblical truths, led her to achieving a Bachelor's degree in Theology, a Master's degree in Biblical Studies, and a Doctor of Religious Studies from Trinity College of the Bible and Theological Seminary. Dr. Gwynne also received a Doctor of Philosophy from Cranmer Memorial Bible College and Seminary.

Lightning Source UK Ltd.
Milton Keynes UK
UKHW010633200121
377380UK00001B/182